Academic Writing for Interna
Students of Science

Academic Writing for International Students of Science will help international students to develop their command of academic scientific writing in English. It guides students through the writing process itself and will help them to produce clear, well-written and well-organised essays and reports. The book covers a range of issues, such as how to explain complex ideas clearly and concisely, how to develop a coherent argument and how to avoid plagiarism by making effective reference to sources.

Through detailed analysis of authentic scientific texts, the book will enhance students' understanding of the nature of academic scientific writing. This will enable them to understand how language and discourse function in a real scientific context. The texts serve as models of good writing and are followed by practice activities which will help students to develop their own writing skills.

Key topics include:

- the writing process;
- academic scientific style;
- sentence structure;
- paragraph development;
- referring to sources;
- coherence, argument and critical thinking;
- academic and scientific conventions.

This book will be an invaluable companion to those studying for a science or technology degree in an English-speaking institution. Informative study boxes, model answers and a clear, comprehensive answer key mean that the book can be used for self-study or with guidance in the classroom.

Jane Bottomley is a Senior Language Tutor at the University of Manchester. She has worked as a writer and editor on a number of books, websites and dictionaries.

Academic Writing for International Students of Science

Jane Bottomley

Routledge
Taylor & Francis Group

LONDON AND NEW YORK

First published 2015
by Routledge
2 Park Square, Milton Park, Abingdon, Oxon OX14 4RN

and by Routledge
711 Third Avenue, New York, NY 10017

Routledge is an imprint of the Taylor & Francis Group, an informa business

British Library Cataloguing in Publication Data
A catalogue record for this book is available from the British Library

Library of Congress Cataloging-in-Publication Data
A catalog record for this book has been requested.

ISBN: 978-0-415-83240-3 (hbk)
ISBN: 978-0-415-83241-0 (pbk)
ISBN: 978-1-315-77805-1 (ebk)

Typeset in Galliard
by Cenveo Publisher Services

Contents

Acknowledgements

My thanks to the many students, friends and colleagues who have contributed in a number of ways to the development of these materials.

Particular thanks are owed to the following: Michael Burton, cousin and chemist, for his invaluable support, sound advice and detailed assessment of the work in progress; John Morley, Ian Pople, Rob Marks and Vanesa Rodriguez Juiz for their careful scrutiny of various chapters, and excellent suggestions for improvements. Thanks are also due to: Ros Cranston, Sue Boswell-Rees, Phil Leeke and Jenny White for their useful feedback; Joy Baugh for kindly allowing me to use her idea for predicting references; June O'Brien for her idea for the task on reordering information; Mark Whitely for his patient explanations of chemistry; Frances Nicholson and Pat Campbell for their kind support.

I would also like to thank the students, skilled writers all, who very generously allowed me to use their work in progress in this book: Sarmed A. Salih; Astone Nanja; Parikshit Deshmukh; Jing Yan. I am also grateful to Victoria Konstantinidi for her keen interest, and helpful ideas on the learner's perspective.

My thanks also to Natasha Ellis-Knight and Philip Mudd at Routledge for their careful guidance.

Introduction

This book is designed to help you, as an international student of science, to develop your command of English language and discourse. It will enable you to produce writing of a high standard, thus helping you to complete written assignments successfully.

You will acquire knowledge, skills and strategies to help you produce writing which is accurate, well-expressed, clear and coherent. You will also reflect on the nature of analysis, argument and critical thinking, all of which give depth to academic writing. In addition, you will learn how to refer to sources effectively, and to employ a range of conventions associated with academic scientific writing.

You will look at the writing process itself, study the mechanics of writing, i.e. grammar and punctuation, and explore the characteristics of academic scientific discourse.

Most example sentences and texts are taken from authentic academic scientific sources, providing you with an opportunity to see how language works in a real-life scientific context. Authentic sources are indicated by references or, in the case of individual sentences or very short texts, by this symbol:

The book adopts a broad view of science which includes the natural sciences, medicine, technology and engineering. Texts have been chosen which are accessible to a general reader.

However, it is advised that you use dictionaries and websites to help you with any difficult words, as this will allow you to focus on the nature of the writing rather than individual words.

There are also a number of texts written by students I have worked with at the University of Manchester, all of which demonstrate the improvements they were able to make as they studied some of the things in this book – in conjunction with their own skills and hard work!

There are a large number of practical activities, including:

- **explorative tasks**, which help you to explore language use and discourse in academic scientific writing, guiding you towards noticing important patterns, and developing a clear understanding of the rules or tendencies which govern these patterns;
- **practice activities**, which allow you to consolidate your understanding of rules and patterns and put them into practice;
- **review tasks**, which provide you with an opportunity to revise the points covered in a chapter by producing a short text.

When an answer is provided in the **Answer Key**, this symbol is used:

Sometimes answers are included within a chapter after the task, like this:

For some tasks, you are required to produce a text. If you are using this book in class, you may be able to get feedback on your text from a teacher. If you are using this book for self-study, the **Model Texts** will help you see what can be achieved, and provide you with some language and ideas that you can use in the future.

The book includes a number of **Study Boxes** like this:

Study Box

These provide you with guidance to help you complete the tasks, as well as highlighting key language points and study strategies.

The book works as both a textbook that you can work through chapter by chapter, and as a reference that you can dip into when you want to focus on a particular area, or need a particular piece of information.

The symbol

refers you to related areas in other chapters and in the appendices.

The flag symbol alerts you to key points to note in a particular area of study:

I have developed the activities in this book over a number of years, working closely with many students studying, or preparing to study, in the science departments of the University of Manchester. Many of those students found these activities helpful in their development as writers, and produced some excellent work along the way – some of which features in this book! These students also helped me to improve the materials with their astute comments. It is hoped that we have created materials which you will enjoy using and find useful in your own development as a writer.

The writing process

As a student of science, it is easy to become absorbed by the research process – the investigation of the literature, or the work you are doing in the lab, for instance. This is a good thing of course, but it can sometimes lead you to put off the actual writing up of your work until the last minute. For most students, this does not produce good results. Writing is a process, involving various stages, and it takes a lot of time and effort to produce a text which is clear, readable and professional. For university science students like you, this process starts with an assignment which will require you to demonstrate your knowledge and understanding of a particular area of science, or to detail your own scientific investigation. This chapter will guide you through the writing process, and show you how to fully engage with it in order to complete assignments successfully.

2.1 Writing to develop and communicate thinking

The link between thinking and writing is often underestimated.

Explorative Task

Look at the views of the two experienced scientists and educators expressed below, and answer the questions that follow.

The power of writing as an aid in thinking is not often appreciated. Everyone knows that someone who writes successfully gets his thoughts completely in order before he publishes. But it is seldom pointed out that the very act of writing can help to clarify thinking. Put down woolly thoughts on paper, and their woolliness is immediately exposed. If students come to realise this, they will write willingly and frequently at all stages of their work, instead of relegating "writing up" to the very end and regarding it as a dreadful chore that has little to do with their "real" work.

(Peter Woodford, in 'Sounder thinking through clearer writing', 1967: 744)

[Writing's] the best way to organise thoughts and to try and put things in as perfect and elegant a way as you can. A lot of scientists hate writing. Most scientists love being in the lab and doing the work and when the work is done, they're finished. Writing is a chore. It's something they have to do to get the work out. They do it with resentment. But conceptually to them, it is not part of the creative process. I don't look at it that way at all. When I get the results, I can't wait to write them up. That's the synthesis. It's the exploration of the consequences and meaning.

(Stephen Jay Gould, in Dreifus, 1999)

1. Do you enjoy writing, or do you see it as a 'chore' (a necessary, but unpleasant task)?
2. Do you look forward to writing about what you have found out in the lab or in the literature, or do you put it off until the last possible minute?
3. Has a teacher or lecturer ever told you that they did not follow what you were saying in a piece of writing, or that the writing was 'woolly', i.e. unclear, vague or ambiguous?
4. Do you consciously use the writing process to help you improve your understanding of the science?

The more you use the writing process to clarify your own thinking, the clearer your writing will be for the reader. The person reading (and assessing!) your work does not just want to see scientific facts, they want to see your 'thinking', i.e. your analysis and reasoning, developed on the page.

2.2 Reflecting on your current approach to writing

In order to develop as a writer, it is necessary to reflect on your current approach to writing and to consider if you are doing all you can to produce writing of a high standard.

2.2.1 Preparing to write

The way you prepare for a written assignment will help to determine the quality of the final text.

Explorative Task

Reflect on your current approach to writing by completing the table.

	Always	Sometimes	Never
I analyse the assignment in detail, highlighting **key phrases**.			
I note down (or '**brainstorm**') what I already know about the topic.			
I think carefully about the **purpose** of the text and the **expectations** of the person reading it and assessing it.			
I think carefully about constraints of time and space, i.e. the **deadline** and the **word limit**.			
I produce a **provisional outline**, i.e. a plan of work, including what I expect to cover, some sense of organisation which reflects how the different sub topics relate to each other, and some key references linked to each part.			
I consider alternative outlines.			
I think carefully about how to **identify and evaluate sources**.			
I take notes or highlight/annotate sources.			
I reassess my own ideas, approach and outline in the light of what I have read.			

Study Box: Improving your approach to research and writing

1) Use the tools provided by your university library website to focus your literature search.

   These sites have tools to limit your search to the most popular or most recent books and articles, for example.

   They will also link to the most relevant scientific databases for your subject, such as *Web of Knowledge* or *SciFinder*.

continued . . .

cont.

The books and articles you find in this way will be reliable, in the sense that they are 'peer-reviewed' by authorities in the field.

Websites should be used with care. The websites of official scientific organisations such as *The Royal Society*, are considered to be authoritative sources. There may also be good reason for you to refer to the information provided by international bodies such as *The United Nations*, and official government websites. Most other websites, including media and commercial websites, may be useful but should be treated with caution. *Wikipedia* should only ever be used as very general background reading.

2) Use the following to help you decide if a source is likely to be relevant and useful: the 'blurb' (information on the back cover) and contents pages of a book; the abstract of a journal article, together with its introduction and conclusion.

3) Do not dive into the literature before you have given yourself time to assess the purpose of the assignment. It is easy to become overwhelmed by the reading if you approach it without a clear focus.

4) Before reading, ask yourself what you expect to find out from a particular source.

5) Decide on the best way to make notes for you personally – a linear structure, or a diagram or table. Diagrams and tables can help you to synthesise information from different sources, allowing you to organise information around ideas and arguments, rather than just individual sources.

6) Be prepared to modify and refine your outline as you write, as your understanding and ideas develop. Make sure that the outline reflects your analysis and reasoning, and that it is not simply a patchwork of the literature.

7) As well as adding to your plan, consider if you may need to cut something because it is redundant, irrelevant or takes you above the word limit. You must be selective about what to include. Do not include something just because you have read about it or done a lot of work on it. It is to be expected that some reading will turn out to be irrelevant or insufficiently important, or that it will simply inform what you write without needing to be referred to directly.

Also remember that the word limit is there partly to test your ability to write concisely (▶ **3.1.2**). More is not always better!

8) When you add/remove something from your outline, or reorganise your points, reassess the whole thing to make sure you have not destroyed the **coherence** of your analysis or argument. ▶ **Chapter 8**

Practice: Deciding on an outline

1) *Look at the following essay question and highlight the key phrases.*

   Discuss the impact of portable devices such as laptops, tablets and mobile phones on the way university students conduct their studies.

2) *Brainstorm some ideas (Figure 2.1).*

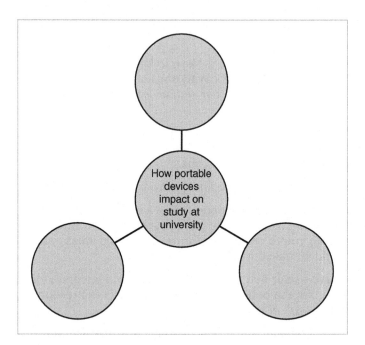

Figure 2.1 Brainstorm some ideas

3) *Think of ways to organise your ideas in a logical way. Experiment with more than one organising principle.*

4) *Compare your organisation and ideas to the three alternative outlines below.*

Outline 1	Outline 2	Outline 3
Type of device	*Uses*	*Positive and negative impacts*
laptops 1. Used for note-taking in lectures. 2. _____ **tablets** 1. Light so can be used on field trips. 2. _____ **mobile phones** 1. Used for photographing board or PowerPoint slides in lectures. (Limited use? Substitute for notes? Quality?) 2. _____	**lectures** 1. Note-taking can be done on laptops. 2. _____ **language skills** 1. Mobile phones allow quick and easy access to electronic dictionaries. 2. _____ **Virtual Learning Environments (VLEs) – facilitate access to course information and promote independent learning** Portable devices enable easy access.	**positive** 1. Easy access to VLEs, which facilitate access to course information and promote independent learning. 2. Smart phones can be used to record lectures. 3. _____ **negative** 1. Not all students happy to use VLEs so much. (Prefer face-to-face contact?) 2. Mobile phones can be a distraction. 3. _____

Note that the same points can often be made regardless of the outline, but the way you fit these points into your overall discussion differs. Experiment until you find an outline that matches how you want to drive the discussion forward.

5) *Add your own ideas to the table above in the spaces provided.*

6) *Write a provisional outline for your essay, or adapt one of the above.*

7) *Consider which facts and figures (evidence) would add depth and interest to your ideas, and think about where you could find these.*

2.2.2 Putting down words on the page

The way you build your sentences, paragraphs and texts can greatly affect the impression you ultimately make on the reader.

Explorative Task

Reflect on your current approach to writing by completing the table.

	Always	Sometimes	Never
I stop frequently to read what I have written to reflect on content and organisation, **editing and redrafting** the text to make improvements.			
I try to put myself in the position of **the reader** and ask myself if they will follow, i.e. check that what I have written **makes sense**.			
I ask myself if I am really **demonstrating my understanding of the science**.			
I revisit my original outline to firm it up or modify it.			

Study Box: Writing up

1) Do not underestimate how much you will need to read and edit as you write. Academics often find that they do this more as they become more experienced writers, not less! Try to imagine the reader's experience as he or she moves through your text.

Reading aloud can be a useful strategy – it can help you decide if something sounds natural and flows easily from point to point.

2) When asking yourself if you have demonstrated a good understanding of the science, ask yourself if you need to go back to the literature, or discuss the ideas with someone.

2.3 The importance of redrafting

Experienced writers often produce several drafts of a text before they feel happy with it. It is important that you edit and redraft your work as you write to make it as clear and readable as possible.

Explorative Task

Read the student's two drafts. Which one is easier to read? Complete the table which follows to help you think about why this might be. 🔑

Text A

The Third Generation Partnership Project (3GPP) defined two parts of 3G evolution standards: High Speed Packet Access (HSPA) and Long Term Evolution (LTE) [1]. Both HSPA and LTE have advantages and disadvantages. There are many factors affecting the decision of operators to choose the appropriate evolution standard, such cost and performance [1]. This will be likely to influence operator's decision on network architecture. In this essay, an overview of 3G technology is outlined. Following this, the merits and demerits of each evolution standard are discussed and some advices are given.

Text B

In order to enable existing mobile systems to meet the requirements of modern high-tech development, two 3G evolution standards, as defined by the Third Generation Partnership Project (3GPP), have been proposed: High Speed Packet Access (HSPA) and Long Term Evolution (LTE) [1]. Operators must decide on the most suitable evolution standard for their network; there are a number of factors which will influence this decision, such as cost and performance [1]. Both HSPA and LTE have advantages and disadvantages, as has been documented in the literature [1]. The purpose of this essay is to examine the merits and demerits of HSPA and LTE. The first section provides an overview of 3G technology. This is followed by a discussion of the recent research into the differences between the two evolution standards, along with some recommendations for future practice in the industry.

Which text	Text A	Text B
begins with a clear contextualisation of current developments in the field (mobile systems)?		
introduces the ideas in a logical, step-by-step fashion?		
has a clearer outline of what is to follow in the rest of the essay?		
has fewer grammatical errors and more natural expression?		

2.4 Focus on proofreading

Do not confuse editing/redrafting and proofreading.

Editing and redrafting involves changing content, organisation of information and expression as you process knowledge and develop ideas; this is the process through which you improve clarity and coherence.

Proofreading is surface-level checking of grammar and punctuation; this can be done to some degree whilst writing, but there should always be detailed proofreading of the final text when you are fairly sure you do not want to make substantial changes to content and organisation.

Practice

Correct the mistakes in grammar and punctuation in the text.

> Most universities has Virtual Learning Environments (VLEs) such as blackboard
> and moodle. It provide online space for course modules where students can access
> informations on course content, assessment, further study. VLE are also used for
> the electronic submission of assessed work, that enables lecturers to use software
> such as turnitin to check for plagiarism in student's work. A further function of VLEs
> is to provide a space for students enter into discussion with each other. Whilst this
> would appear to be an excellent opportunity for all students to develop their idea
> and understanding, and for non-native speakers to practice their language skills, it
> would seem that many are reluctant to engage in this type of activity, the reasons of
> this remain unclear.

▶   Model Text 1, Appendix 4

▶   **Chapter 4** for information on sentence structure and sentence boundaries

▶   **4.2.4** for information on relative clauses

▶   **5.2** for information on punctuation

▶ **9.8** for information on spelling

▶ **Appendix 2** for information on nouns and articles

▶ **Appendix 3** for common errors

Many people ask a native speaker to 'check' their writing, or employ someone to do this. There is nothing wrong with this in principle, but be aware that this should ideally take place at the proofreading stage, when you are satisfied with the overall content and organisation. It is your responsibility to make your writing clear and coherent, and, anyway, you are unlikely to find someone who is an expert in your scientific field, so it would be unwise (as well as unethical!) to ask them to do anything which would change the content or organisation of your text; the native speaker's role should be to check for surface errors in grammar and punctuation, or to make the phraseology more natural and idiomatic – without changing your meaning.

Academic scientific style

This chapter will help you to become familiar with the features of good academic scientific style, focussing firstly on the importance of clarity, and secondly on the language and conventions associated with this style of writing.

3.1 Clarity

[N]o one who has something original or important to say will willingly run the risk of being misunderstood; people who write obscurely are either unskilled in writing or up to mischief.

(Peter Medawar, 1974, in Dawkins, 2008: 183)

Although the scientific content of a text may be complex and difficult to understand, the text itself should be as clear and readable as possible. Many factors contribute to clarity, some of which are covered in other parts of the book. (See links ▶ to other chapters.) In this chapter, you will focus on sentence length, text organisation, and being concise and precise.

3.1.1 Sentence length and text organisation

Sentence length and text organisation can greatly affect clarity.

Explorative Task

Read the two texts. Which one is easier to read? Match the texts to one of the descriptions in the table which follows to help you think about why this might be.

Text A

Telecommunications engineering is a discipline that brings together electrical
engineering and computer science in order to enhance telecommunications
systems. The work involved ranges from basic circuit design to strategic mass
developments. The work of a telecommunications engineer includes designing
and overseeing the installation of telecommunications equipment such as complex
electronic switching systems, copper wire telephone facilities and fibre optics.

Text B

The discipline of telecommunications engineering, including the designing and installation
overseeing of telecommunications equipment and facilities, such as complex electronic
switching systems, copper wire telephone facilities and fibre optics, is the enhancement
of telecommunication systems through the bringing together of electrical engineering
and computer science, from basic circuit design to strategic mass developments.

1) Text _____	2) Text _____
is one very long sentence.	is broken up into shorter sentences.
has only one main verb. (Underline this.)	has three sentences, each with a main verb. (Underline these.)
gives a general definition near the end of the text, after specific details and examples have been given.	begins with a general definition, followed by specific details and examples.

Study Box: Long or short sentences?

It is sometimes thought that using very long sentences automatically makes a
text 'sound more academic', but this is not necessarily the case. Short sentences
can be used to good effect in scientific writing as they can convey information
very clearly. Long sentences can also be useful as they allow you to combine
information efficiently. But remember that any long sentences used must be
carefully controlled (▶ **Chapters 4** and **5**), and not become a string of loosely
connected words and phrases.

Most scientific writing is usually a combination of long and short sentences.

Many other factors contribute to clarity:

▶ **Chapter 2** to find out about the importance of engaging with the writing process to
clarify thinking and expression

▶ **Chapters 4** and **5**, which focus on the importance of using good sentence structure to achieve clear expression; note the focus on precise punctuation

▶ **Chapters 6** and **8**, which explain how to develop clear paragraphs and texts; note the focus on punctuation

▶ **Chapter 9** to look at how following the conventions of academic and scientific writing can help to make a text easier to follow

Practice

Rewrite this text so that it is clearer.

> Paediatrics is a branch of medicine that deals with the care of infants, children and adolescents, the main differences between paediatric and adult medicine being the differences in physiology and legal status, with children unable to make decisions for themselves. Paediatricians usually deal with children from birth to eighteen years of age.

▶ Model Text 2, Appendix 4

3.1.2 Being concise

Clear scientific language is concise; wordiness and redundancy can be distracting and confusing for the reader, and are often a sign that the writer is not in full control of the development of ideas in a text.

Practice (i)

Rewrite these sentences to make them more concise.

1) All of the studies had limitations.
2) Scientists need to find solutions to solve these problems.
3) He makes a comparison of both the two systems.
4) In the conclusion part of the chapter, she reiterates the importance and significance of the results.
5) Pollution is a global problem throughout the world.

Practice (ii)

1) *Look at the student's first draft and the lecturer's comments which follow.*

> A number of technological methods of extraction of copper are available, which include hydrometallurgy, solvent extraction, liquid-liquid electrochemistry and electrowinning. Liquid–liquid electrochemistry is the focus of this project. Each of these processes is described below and liquid–liquid electrochemistry is given greater consideration as it is the focus of this project.

Accurate and well expressed – could be more concise, however.

2) *Rewrite the text so that it is clear and concise.*
3) *Compare your text with the student's second draft.* ▶ **Model Text 3, Appendix 4**

3.1.3 Being precise

Writing should be concise, but, at the same time, it should be precise and explicit in meaning, avoiding vague expression or ambiguity.

Study Box: Precision in writing

1) Avoid using *etc.* or *and so on*. Use *such as* instead, when you want to give just two or three examples, e.g.

cancer, diabetes, etc. → diseases **such as** cancer and diabetes

2) Avoid vague use of words, particularly prepositions; instead, use common collocations (words which often go together) and fixed phrases with precise meaning, e.g.

For applications, nanotechnology has huge potential.

→ **In terms of** applications, nanotechnology has huge potential.

There are a number of factors of climate.

→ There are a number of **factors affecting** climate.

There are many problems of excessive alcohol consumption.

→ There are many **problems associated with** excessive alcohol consumption.

(= problems that arise when someone consumes too much alcohol)

Compare with:

the problem of excessive alcohol consumption

(= excessive alcohol consumption is a problem)

▨ **Practice**

Identify any vague expressions in these sentences and try to make them more precise and explicit. 🔑

1) The regulations cover the use of oil, gas, etc.
2) Buildings in the city are constructed of concrete, timber and so on.
3) For applications, this polymer is very versatile.
4) There are a number of factors of blood pressure.
5) There are many problems of obesity.

3.2 Language and conventions

There are many forms of writing that can be labelled as 'scientific', including on the one hand, academic textbooks and journals, and on the other, popular science books, newspaper articles and websites. This section will help you to become more familiar with the language and conventions associated with academic style, and to distinguish this type of writing from the journalistic or informal style found elsewhere. You will then complete a number of tasks to help you improve your own style.

3.2.1 What is academic scientific writing?

Academic scientific writing is characterised by a particular style of writing which you should try to adopt in your assignments.

Explorative Task

1) *Read through the texts below quite quickly, without using a dictionary – it is not necessary to understand every word for this task – and decide whether you think they come from an academic or non-academic source.*

Text A

The basic particles of which atoms are composed are the proton, the electron and the neutron. Some key properties of the proton, electron, and neutron are given in Table 1.4. A neutron and a proton have approximately the same mass and, relative to these, the electron has a negligible mass. The charge on a proton is of equal magnitude, but opposite sign, to that on an electron and so the combination of equal numbers of protons and electrons results in an assembly that is neutral overall. A neutron, as its name suggests, is neutral – it has no charge.

Text B

It sounds like an unusual way to win a Nobel Prize.

But ordinary sticky tape was crucial to the breakthrough that yielded graphene, a material with amazing properties and – potentially – numerous practical applications.

Graphene is a flat layer of carbon atoms tightly packed into a two-dimensional honeycomb arrangement.

It is both the thinnest and the strongest material known to science, and it conducts electricity better than copper.

This year's winners of the physics prize, Andre Geim and Konstantin Novoselov, from Manchester University, UK, extracted graphene from the common material known as graphite – widely used as lead in pencils.

Placing the adhesive tape on graphite, they managed to rip off thin flakes of carbon.

In the beginning they got flakes consisting of many layers of graphene.

But as they repeated the process many times, the flakes got thinner.

Text C

Microorganisms are used to recycle water during sewage treatment (Figure 1.7), converting the waste into useful byproducts such as CO_2, nitrates, phosphates, sulphates, ammonia, hydrogen sulphide and methane. Microbes have been routinely used for bioremediation since 1988, cleaning up toxic waste generated in a variety of industrial processes. In these cases, the organisms use the toxic waste as a source of energy, and in the process they decontaminate it. They can also clean up underground wells, chemical spills and oil spills as well as producing useful products such as enzymes that are widely used in cleaning solutions.

Text D

One of Faraday's greatest intellectual innovations was the idea of force fields. These days, thanks to books and movies about bug-eyed aliens and their starships, most people are familiar with the term, so maybe he should get a royalty. But in the centuries between Newton and Faraday one of the great mysteries of physics was that its laws seemed to indicate that forces act across the empty space that separates interacting objects. Faraday didn't like that. He believed that to move an object, something has to come in contact with it. And so he imagined the space between electric charges and magnets as being filled with invisible tubes that physically do the pushing and pulling. Faraday called those tubes a force field.

Text E

Buildings in the city of Adapazari, Turkey, suffered heavy damage during the 1999 Marmara earthquake. Much of the devastation was attributed to the failure of the low plasticity non-plastic silts (Donahue *et al*. 2007) that had been deposited by the Sakarya River in its almost annual flooding of the plain over the past 7,000 years (Bol *et al*. 2010). The flood waters often did not recede for a considerable time, and they occasionally formed lakes.

Text F

In December, philosopher and artificial intelligence expert Aaron Sloman announced his intention to create nothing less than a robot mathematician. He reckons he has identified a key component of how humans develop mathematical talent. If he's right, it should be possible to program a machine to be as good as us at mathematics, and possibly better.

Sloman's creature is not meant to be a mathematical genius capable of advancing the frontiers of mathematical knowledge: his primary aim, outlined in the journal *Artificial Intelligence* (vol 172, p2015), is to improve our understanding of where our mathematical ability comes from. Nevertheless, it is possible that such a robot could take us beyond what mathematicians have achieved so far. Forget robot vacuum cleaners and android waitresses; we're talking about a machine that could spawn a race of cyber-nerds capable of creating entirely new forms of mathematics.

Text G

Recently, Flaherty *et al.*[9] published the results of a questionnaire on older outpatients' use of alternative therapies in the US and Japan. According to their data, 74.3% of older Japanese outpatients had used at least one alternative therapy in the past 12 months: 22.0% had used herbs, 7.3% had used acupuncture, and 5.3% had used chiropractic.

Text H

Overweight and obesity are major threats to public health globally. One estimate suggests that 1.46 billion adults worldwide were overweight in 2008,[1] and projections suggest that by 2020 over 70% of adults in the United Kingdom and United States will be overweight.[2] This is likely to result in millions of additional cases of diabetes and heart disease and thousands of additional cases of cancer.[2]

2) *What differences do you notice between the academic and non-academic texts? Some of these differences will be explored in the following section.*

3.2.2 Common features of academic scientific texts

The academic texts in **3.2.1** are characterised by certain language and conventions.

Explorative Task

Match the features of academic scientific writing style (A) to examples of language and conventions in the examples (B) taken from the texts in **3.2.1.**

A
Language and conventions

1) Academic scientific texts use **careful, cautious** language when necessary, in order to avoid making overgeneralisations.

    Find examples of cautious language: _____

2) They tend to adopt an **impersonal** style, making use of passive constructions (▶ **Appendix 1**), and mostly avoiding the use of the personal pronouns *I, we* and *you.*

    Find examples of passive constructions: _____

3) They use **scientific/technical terminology** and a **neutral/formal** tone, avoiding the colloquial or highly stylised language sometimes found in popular science books, journalism and websites.

    *Find five examples of scientific/technical terms:*_____

4) They use **careful punctuation**, making effective use of colons and semi-colons to organise ideas (▶ **5.2** and **5.3**), and mostly avoiding informal punctuation devices such as contractions, dashes and exclamation marks.

Find an example of colon use: _____

5) They contain **references** to sources, following standard referencing conventions (▶ **9.1**). They tend not to include detailed bibliographic information in the main text, as is often the case in popular science writing.

Find examples of two styles of academic referencing: _____

6) They follow established **conventions** with regard to the use of tables and figures. (▶ **Chapter 9** for more information on academic and scientific conventions)

Find examples of references to tables and figures: _____

B
Example Texts

a) A neutron and a proton have **approximately** the same mass ...
b) This is **likely** to result in millions of additional cases of diabetes and heart disease and thousands of additional cases of cancer.[2]
c) Some key properties of the proton, electron, and neutron **are given** in **Table 1.4**.
d) According to their data, 74.3% of older Japanese outpatients had used at least one alternative therapy in the past 12 months: 22.0% had used herbs, 7.3% had used acupuncture, and 5.3% had used chiropractic.
e) ... deposited by the Sakarya River in its almost annual flooding of the plain over the past 7,000 years **(Bol *et al.* 2010)**.
f) **Much of** the devastation **has been attributed** to the failure of the low plasticity non-plastic silts ...
g) Microorganisms **are used** to recycle water during sewage treatment **(Figure 1.7)** ...

Note that the line between academic and non-academic texts is not always clearly drawn. As you can see from the texts in **3.2.1**, academic texts contain occasional informal features such as dashes, e.g.

A neutron, as its name suggests, is neutral – it has no charge.

and the non-academic texts can be academic in tone, e.g.

Graphene is a flat layer of carbon atoms tightly packed into a two-dimensional honeycomb arrangement.

Furthermore, in modern textbooks (including this one!), and some academic journals, informal devices such as contractions and personal pronouns are often employed to make the text more accessible.

While it is good to be aware of the variation in style across academic scientific texts, you should follow the formal conventions outlined above as far as possible in your own academic work, unless otherwise specified, and you should certainly avoid colloquial expressions.

Study Box: Increasing formality

1) Use the formal negatives *no/little/few*, e.g.

    At the time, not many women worked in this area of science.

    → At the time, **few** women worked in this area of science.

    Not much research has been carried out on this topic.

    → **Little** research has been carried out on this topic.

Note that *few* is used with countable nouns and *little* with uncountable nouns.

Be careful not to confuse with *a few/a little*, meaning *some* or *a small number/amount*.

▶ **Appendix 3, 2.2** on *fewer* and *less*

2) Place adverbs before the main verb, rather than at the beginning (or sometimes the end) of a sentence, as is common in spoken English, e.g.

    Originally, the research was conducted in China.

    → The research was **originally** conducted in China.

    Then the tube was placed in the furnace.

    → The tube was **then** placed in the furnace.

3) Note that, in academic texts, it is generally considered better to avoid the use of *and* and *but* at the start of a sentence.

4) Avoid informal expressions such as *get, about, though* and *like*, e.g.

    Brown got a Nobel Prize for his work on boranes.

    → Brown **received/earned/was awarded** a Nobel Prize for his work on boranes.

    about 200 people

    → **approximately/an estimated** 200 people

    Though cooking may destroy the bacterial cells, it is unlikely to inactivate the toxin.

    → **Although** cooking may destroy the bacterial cells, it is unlikely to inactivate the toxin.

    devices like smart phones and tablets

    → devices **such as** smart phones and tablets

5) Avoid informal uses of *do/make/get* by choosing more formal equivalents:

    get worse → *deteriorate*
    make easier → *facilitate*
    do better → *improve*

continued . . .

cont.

> 6) Be careful when using *besides* and *as well*. Used alone, they have an informal tone; in academic writing, they should be followed by a noun or *–ing* form, e.g.
>
> The dye is used in the textile industry. Besides, it has applications in food production.
>
> → **Besides being used** in the textile industry, the dye has applications in food production.
>
> The dye has applications in the food industry as well.
>
> → **As well as being used** in the textile industry, the dye has applications in the food industry.
>
> 7) Avoid conversational expressions such as *actually*, *by the way* or *to be honest*.
> 8) Avoid the informal expressions *more and more* and *a lot of/lots of*, e.g.
>
> A lot of studies back up these findings.
>
> → **Many/A large number of/A considerable number of** studies back up these findings.
>
> The above expressions should only be used with countable nouns; use the expressions below with uncountable nouns:
>
> **a large amount of/a considerable amount of/a great deal of** time/money/research

Practice (i)

Identify examples of informal style in these examples from **3.2.1.**

1) ... we're talking about a machine that could spawn a race of cyber-nerds ...
2) It sounds like an unusual way to win a Nobel Prize.
3) ... they got flakes consisting of many layers of graphene ...
4) ... bug-eyed aliens and their starships ...
5) He reckons he has identified a key component of how humans develop mathematical talent.
6) And so he imagined the space between electric charges and magnets as being filled with invisible tubes that physically do the pushing and pulling.
7) ... a material with amazing properties and – potentially – numerous practical applications ...
8) Faraday didn't like that.
9) ... Andre Geim and Konstantin Novoselov, from Manchester University, UK ...
10) ... his primary aim, outlined in the journal *Artificial Intelligence* (vol 172, p 2015) ...

Practice (ii)

Which of these sentences, a or b, would be better in an academic text? Why? Note that all the sentences are grammatically correct, and could possibly feature in academic texts, but one is more academic in style than the other.

1)
   a)   The first clinical trial was conducted in 2008.
   b)   We conducted the first clinical trial in 2008.

2)
   a)   There are three main treatments for cancer – surgery, radiation therapy and
        chemotherapy.
   b)   There are three main treatments for cancer: surgery, radiation therapy and
        chemotherapy.

3)
   a)   Mobile phone use poses a danger to health.
   b)   Mobile phone use may pose a danger to health.

4)
   a)   Not many materials exhibit strong magnetism.
   b)   Few materials exhibit strong magnetism.

5)
   a)   Rutherford received the Nobel Prize in Chemistry in 1908.
   b)   Rutherford got the Nobel Prize in Chemistry in 1908.

6)
   a)   There are about 3000 species of cricket in the world.
   b)   There are approximately 3000 species of cricket in the world.

7)
   a)   An increasing number of seals are being treated for internal problems caused by oil
        poisoning.
   b)   More and more seals are being treated for internal problems caused by oil poisoning.

8)
   a)   The machine was originally developed for internal company research.
   b)   Originally, the machine was developed for internal company research.

Practice (iii)

*Rewrite these sentences to make them more academic in style. Most sentences only require
minor changes.*

1)   In the beginning they got flakes consisting of many layers of graphene.
     But as they repeated the process many times, the flakes got thinner.
     _____

2)   He reckons he has identified a key component of how humans develop mathematical
     talent.
     _____

3)   This study aims to figure what caused the structural damage.
     _____

4)   A lot of research has been done on the subject of runway friction.
     _____

5)   Most thermometers are closed glass tubes containing liquids like alcohol or mercury.
     _____

6) Then, the solution was heated to about 70°C.

_____

7) You can see the results of the analysis in Table 2.

_____

8) Not much is known about the proteins linked with RNA.

_____

9) Eating disorders cause individuals to feel tired and depressed.

_____

10) There are three different types of volcano – active volcanoes (erupt frequently), dormant volcanoes (temporarily inactive but not fully extinct), and extinct volcanoes (unlikely to erupt again).

_____

Review Task

Summarise the information in Text B in **3.2.1**, presenting it in a more academic style. You will need to think about organisation of information as well as language. Use your own words as much as possible, but do not try to change technical expressions. ▶ **Chapter 7** _for more information on this_

▶ **Model Text 4, Appendix 4**

CHAPTER

4

Sentence structure 1

In order to express yourself clearly, you need to have good control of sentence structure. This chapter will help you to write clear sentences with good grammar and punctuation.

4.1 Subject + verb structures

Most sentences in English are built around one or more $\overset{S}{\textbf{subject}} + \overset{V}{\textbf{verb}}$ structures, where the verb agrees with the subject, e.g.

- $\overset{S}{\overline{\textbf{Heat capacity}}} \overset{V}{\overline{\textbf{is}}}$ the ability to absorb and retain heat.

- $\overline{\textbf{Deformation of concrete}} \overset{S}{\underline{\hspace{1.5em}}} \overline{\textbf{results}} \overset{V}{\underline{\hspace{1em}}}$ both from environmental effects, such as moisture gain or loss and heat, and from applied stress, both long- and short-term.

- $\overset{S}{\overline{\textbf{Bacteria}}} \overset{V}{\overline{\textbf{are}}}$ the smallest living organisms.

- $\overset{S}{\overline{\textbf{Atoms}}}$, the building blocks of elements, $\overset{V}{\overline{\textbf{consist}}}$ of a nucleus surrounded by a cloud of orbiting electrons.

$$\text{S}$$

- The concepts underlying the changing health needs, status and situations of groups

  $$\text{V}$$

  $$\text{S}$$

  and nations are becoming ever better understood, and terms to describe them

  $$\text{V}$$

  are changing.

Note that the subject can be made up of one or several words.

▶ **Appendix 2** on **Noun Phrases** for information on the structure of multi-word subjects

There are certain verb forms and patterns which are common in academic scientific writing.

▶ **Appendix 1** on **Verb Forms and Patterns**

Explorative Task

*Identify the **subject + verb** structures in these sentences.*

1) Lime (CaO) is widely used as an ingredient in mortars, plasters and masonry.
2) One of the most noticeable trends over many decades has been shifting patterns of health and especially the causes of morbidity (illness) and mortality (death).
3) A motherboard is the major circuit board inside a computer and it holds the processor, the computer bus, the main memory and many other vital components.
4) Solar power is one facet of renewable energy, with wind and geothermal being others.
5) Although quarantine is the oldest method of dealing with communicable diseases, it is now generally used only for very severe diseases, such as cholera and yellow fever.

4.2 Sentence types

In English, **subject + verb** structures occur in three main types of sentence.

Explorative Task

*Look again at some of the sentences from **4.1**.*

- *Which has more than one **subject + verb** structure?*
- *How are they linked together? What is the relationship between the two parts of the sentence?*

1) Bacteria are the smallest living organisms.
2) A motherboard is the major circuit board inside a computer and it holds the processor, the computer bus, the main memory and many other vital components.
3) Although quarantine is the oldest method of dealing with communicable diseases, it is now generally used only for very severe diseases, such as cholera and yellow fever.

> The three main sentence types exemplified here are: **simple** (1) (with only one subject + verb structure), **compound** (2) and **complex** (3) (both with two subject + verb structures). These sentence types will be discussed in more detail in the following sections.

4.2.1 Forming simple sentences

Simple sentences consist of a single **main clause**, i.e. they are built around a single **subject + verb** structure. As well as containing a **subject**, and a **verb** which agrees with the subject, a main clause can also contain:

- an **object** (who or what is affected by the verb), e.g.
  o The university funded **the study**.
  o The group researched **the causes of diabetes**.
- a **complement** (information about the subject or object of the clause), e.g.
  o She is **a doctor**.
  o They made him **head of department**.
- an **adverbial** (information about the situation), e.g.
  o The book has **undoubtedly** contributed to the debate on climate change.
  o **In the early 20th century**, many advances were made in the field of physics.
  o **When conducting trials on mice**, they found the drug to be effective and harmless.

> Note that subjects, objects and complements are usually nouns, or rather noun phrases (with more than one word). However, some other elements, such as subordinate clauses (▶ 4.2.2 for an explanation of subordinate clauses), can also take on this function, e.g.
>
> **What Darwin did** changed the way we understand biology.
>
> Also note from the above examples that adverbs, prepositional phrases and subordinate clauses can function as adverbials.

Explorative Task (i)

*Underline extra words or phrases that have been added to the main **subject + verb** structure in each of the simple sentences below. What is the grammar/function of these words and phrases?*

1) Temperatures rose.
2) Temperatures rose steadily.
3) Average temperatures in the south of the country rose steadily.
4) In the period from 2003 to 2013, average temperatures in the south of the country rose steadily.

Explorative Task (ii)

These sentences are not accurately formed. Can you identify the problems with them?

1) It undoubtedly true that computational simulations should not completely replace experimentation.
2) An ICT system is a set-up consists of hardware, software, data, and the people who use these things.
3) Vitamin D is important for the absorption and use of calcium and phosphorus by the body, it is essential for the formation and health of bones, teeth and cartilage.

4.2.2 Compound and complex sentences

As previously mentioned, compound and complex sentences contain two **subject + verb** structures, i.e. **clauses**, but combine them in different ways.

Explorative Task

*Look again at these sentences from **4.1**.*

* *In which sentence could the two clauses exist independently?*
* *In which sentence is one clause (which?) dependent on the other?*

1) A motherboard is the major circuit board inside a computer and it holds the processor, the computer bus, the main memory and many other vital components.
2) Although quarantine is the oldest method of dealing with communicable diseases, it is now generally used only for very severe diseases, such as cholera and yellow fever.

In 1), two facts are combined, but they are not dependent on each other here.
If the sentence were split into two, there would be no change of meaning.
They are independent **main clauses** joined by a **coordinating conjunction**, *and*, to form a **compound sentence**.

In 2), the **subordinating conjunction** *although* introduces a dependent **subordinate clause**, which must be connected to a **main clause** for the sentence to make sense: the two facts (quarantine is the oldest method; it is not widely used now) are related here to form a **complex sentence**. If the subordinating element is removed, the link between the facts is not explicit.

A **compound-complex** sentence contains both coordinated and subordinated clauses, e.g.

•   main clause 1   coordinator   main clause 2

Vaccines against malaria have been sought for years but these have yet to be successful,

subordinate clause

although optimism surfaces regularly.

Study Box: Avoiding common errors in compound and complex sentences

1) Be careful not to duplicate conjunctions, e.g.

   As some of the drug's side effects may be difficult to detect **and** patients might take a long time to become aware of them. ✗

   As some of the drug's side effects may be difficult to detect, patients might take a long time to become aware of them. ✓

   Some of the drug's side effects may be difficult to detect **and** patients might take a long time to become aware of them. ✓

2) Be careful not to write just half a sentence when using subordinating conjunctions such as *whereas* and *because*, e.g.

   Influenza B and C viruses mainly affect humans. Whereas influenza A viruses infect a range of mammalian and avian species. ✗

   Influenza B and C viruses mainly affect humans, whereas influenza A viruses infect a range of mammalian and avian species. ✓

3) Avoid 'stringy' sentences with lots of *and*s and *but*s. They are wordy, unstructured and difficult to read.

   The weather conditions worsened and this caused a number of problems and there were forest fires and droughts but the long-term effects were limited. ✗

   The weather conditions worsened, which caused a number of problems including forest fires and droughts. However, the long-term effects were limited. ✓

Practice

Correct or improve these sentences.

1) Although the structure of the building was weakened, but experts agreed that there was no danger of it collapsing.

   _____

2) The drug trial was abandoned. Because the side effects were considered to be too serious.

   _____

3) The panda was artificially inseminated and experts claimed that her hormone and behavioural signs indicated that she was carrying a foetus but her behaviour changed and she is thought to have lost the cub.

4.2.2.1 Forming compound sentences

The typical sentence pattern for compound sentences is:

subject + verb (…) + coordinating conjunction (*and/but/or*) + subject + verb (…)

*   A motherboard is the major circuit board inside a computer and it holds the processor, the computer bus, the main memory and many other vital components.

A comma is often used before the conjunction, e.g.

*   Obesity appears to have more negative health consequences than smoking, drinking or poverty, and it also affects more people.

In compound sentences, when both clauses have the same subject, the subject of the second clause can be omitted, e.g.

*   Glass is resistant to most chemicals but can be dissolved by hydrofluoric acid.

However, it should be retained if there is any chance of ambiguity.

Practice

Link the sentence halves with the right coordinating conjunction to form compound sentences.

1) A poor diet can lead to obesity	and	a)	it has also brought with it a number of problems.
2) The hurricane destroyed a number of buildings	but	b)	injected.
	or	c)	others show little improvement.
3) The drug can be taken orally		d)	cause a number of health problems.
4) The Internet has improved our lives in many ways		e)	caused major damage to trees.
5) Some patients respond well to therapy			

1) _____

2) _____

3) _____

4) _____

5) _____

4.2.2.2 *Forming complex sentences with subordinating conjunctions*

Typical sentence patterns when using **subordinating conjunctions** are:

subordinating conjunction + subject + verb (...), + subject + verb (...)

(clauses usually separated by comma)

subordinate clause   main clause

* As soon as the liquid reaches the required temperature, it should be removed from the heat.

or

subject + verb (...) + subordinating conjunction + subject + verb (...)

(comma not usually used)

main clause   subordinate clause

* The liquid should be removed from the heat as soon as it reaches the required temperature.

Some common examples of **subordinating conjunctions** used in academic writing are:

* Indicating time, duration or sequence: *when; while; as; as soon as; since; until; before; after*
* Stating conditions: *if; unless; in case; provided that*
* Giving reasons: *because; since; as*
* Indicating result: *so; so that*
* Contrasting: *while; whilst; whereas*
* Indicating concession: *although; even though*

▨ Practice (i)

Choose the correct subordinating conjunction.

1) Many people prefer natural remedies to conventional drugs **as/while** they believe natural remedies have fewer side effects.
2) **Because/Whereas** many buildings in the city are built to withstand earthquakes, some are still at considerable risk.
3) **Although/Since** the weather conditions were fairly good, they decided not to proceed with the test flight.
4) Mobile phones should be switched off **unless/in case** they interfere with emergency equipment.
5) Take the drug **as soon as/until** the symptoms occur.

Practice (ii)

Link the sentence halves and insert the correct subordinating conjunction to form complex sentences:

although; while; as; so that; whereas

1) ___ it remains the case that the brain as a whole has limited powers of repair	a) ___ measures may be taken to reduce the likelihood of future incidents.
2) The stability of glass makes disposal difficult	b) it reaches upwards into biology for many of its extraordinary applications.
3) The reasons for developing type 1 diabetes have not been identified	c) ___ some suggest interaction of dietary factors during pregnancy and early neonatal life.
4) ___ chemistry reaches down into physics for its explanations	d) the potential use of stem cells offers new hope for future therapy for degenerative brain diseases.
5) It is sometimes necessary to acquire information regarding the cause of a ceramic fracture	e) ___ it will not readily break down.

1) _____

2) _____

3) _____

4) _____

5) _____

4.2.3 Other complex sentences

There are a number of other subordinating mechanisms which are common in academic writing.

4.2.3.1 Participle clauses

Typical sentence patterns using participles are:

subject + verb (…), ——*ed/ing* (…)

           main clause   participle clause

- The banks of the river burst, leading to serious flooding.

    ——*ed/ing* (…), subject + verb (…)

    participle clause   main clause

- Written in 1859, Darwin's *Origin of Species* revolutionised the study of biology.

Practice

Complete the sentences with one of the verbs below in a suitable form:

prompt; weigh; use; compose

1) The traffic light system is used on the front of packaging to help consumers assess at a glance the fat, saturated fat, sugar and salt content, _____ them to make healthier dietary choices.
2) The brain is a very complex structure, _____ of around one hundred thousand million (i.e. 10^{11}) neurons.
3) _____ matter before it had undergone transformation from one substance to another led to the principal concept that underlies all explanations in chemistry: the *atom*.
4) Inexpensive microelectronic circuits are mass produced by _____ some very ingenious fabrication techniques.

4.2.3.2 Infinitive clauses of purpose

Infinitive clauses of purpose are very common in scientific writing.

Typical sentence patterns are:

subject + verb (…) + infinitive clause

(comma not usually used)

main clause	infinitive clause

- Organic matter can be added to soil to lower the pH.

infinitive clause, + subject + verb (…)

(comma usually used)

infinitive clause	main clause

- To lower the pH of soil, organic matter can be added.

The phrases *in order to* and *so as to* can also be used to introduce purpose.

- **in order to/so as to** lower the pH of soil

 Practice

Link the sentence halves with the right verb to form complex sentences:

1) All structural concrete contains steel reinforcement in the form of bars or welded mesh	to reduce to take to dilute to compensate for to track down	a) the weight and improve the performance of its aircraft.
2) We must understand the transmission mechanisms of infection so that we can interfere with those mechanisms		b) the low tensile strength of concrete.
3) Water is then added		c) suspects, and to analyse the scenes of crimes.
4) Stemming from analytical chemistry is *forensic chemistry*, in which the techniques of analytical chemistry are used for legal purposes		d) the acid to 20–30% and the mixture is again heated to 100°C for 1 hour.
5) Aluminium–lithium alloys have been developed by the aircraft industry		e) effective public health measures.

1) _____

2) _____

3) _____

4) _____

5) _____

This structure can be very useful in the methods section of a research report, often combined with the passive, e.g.

To obtain the correct values of T_s (skin temperature) by compensating for the effects of different radiation sources the following parameters **were supplied** for the camera: ...

In order to allow acclimatisation, the thermograms **were recorded** after a 15 min stay in the respective environment.

To document the recurrence of thermal windows, we further partitioned each body part into three sections ...

To document the relative size of a thermal window and to observe its chronological development we used the software package ImageJ 1.36B ...

To test for the influence of T_a, age, and body weight on T_s, we used linear mixed effect models ...

(Weissenbock *et al.*, 2010: 183)

4.2.3.3 that-*clauses*

Many verbs (also adjectives and nouns) introduce a subordinate clause with the conjunction *that*, e.g.

- The *First Law* of thermodynamics asserts **that** the total energy of the universe is constant and cannot be changed.

It is often possible to omit *that* from the clause, but it is usually a good idea to retain it in academic writing as it can improve clarity.

Practice

Add the word 'that' to these sentences where necessary/preferable.

1) Immunisation requires we understand the immune mechanisms and we design vaccines that will successfully stimulate protection.
2) One estimate suggests 1.46 billion adults worldwide were overweight in 2008,[1] and projections suggest by 2020 over 70% of adults in the United Kingdom and United States will be overweight.
3) It is popularly believed the cells of wood are living cells, but this is certainly not the case.
4) Chemists take a great deal of interest in the rates of chemical reactions as there is little point knowing they can, in principle, generate a substance in a reaction but it would take a millennium to make a milligram.
5) Over time, it is becoming more apparent the earth is virtually a closed system relative to its constituent materials and its resources are finite.

4.2.4 Focus on relative clauses

Relative clauses are very common in academic writing. They are useful in science as they can specify or define a particular object, e.g.

- A heavy metal is one **that has a high relative atomic mass**.

or add information to a statement, e.g.

- Heavy metals, **which include copper, lead, and zinc**, can be a cause of environmental pollution.

They cause difficulty because they are quite complex in terms of grammar and punctuation.

▶ **8.4** for examples of relative clauses in definitions

Explorative Task

Compare the relative clauses highlighted in the text. In what ways do they differ?

Since the start of the industrial revolution in the late 18th century, there has been an exponential increase in our exploitation of materials for use in the technologies **that have driven economic growth and increased the prosperity and living standards in much of the world**. These advances have not, of course, been uniformly experienced owing to the wide variation in political, economic and social conditions in different regions and countries. Much of the growth has only been possible with the associated development and fabrication of infrastructure, **which has required enormous quantities of construction materials with controlled and reliable properties.**

(Domone and Illston, 2010: 535)

Defining or non-defining relative clause?

The first clause is a **defining** (or '**restrictive**') relative clause. It **specifies** only those 'technologies' responsible for these effects; it does not refer to 'technologies' in general. Defining clauses can begin with *that* or *which* (*that* or *who* for people).

The second clause is a **non-defining/non-restrictive** clause. It refers to 'the development and growth of infrastructure' in general, adding some **extra information** rather than specifying a certain part of it. Non-defining clauses must begin with *which* (or *who* for people), and they must be separated from the main clause by a comma/commas.

Practice (i)

Complete the sentences with: that/which/who and, if necessary, a comma/commas.

1) A computer virus is a program _____ can damage your computer.
2) Brisk walking is something _____ many doctors recommend to those _____ are overweight.
3) A marine engineer is someone _____ works with underwater equipment and systems.
4) Vitamin C _____ is also known as ascorbic acid is required by the body for the growth and repair of tissue.
5) Global warming leads to climate change _____ will ultimately affect people all over the world.

Sometimes, the relative pronoun of a defining relative clause can be omitted if it refers to the object, rather than the subject of a sentence. Compare:

* technologies that have driven economic growth
* technologies (that) industry has employed

Can any of the relative pronouns in the sentences in **Practice (i)** *be omitted?*

Relative clauses can also sometimes be further reduced (to form 'reduced relative clauses'), i.e. both the relative pronoun and auxiliary verb *to be* can be omitted, leaving just a past participle, e.g.

- This study shows that neither recipes **created** by popular television chefs nor ready meals **produced** by three leading UK supermarket chains meet national or international nutritional standards for a balanced diet.
- Highly educated people **living** in urban areas use more dietary supplements.

Can any of the sentences in **Practice (i)** *be reduced?*

Relative clauses with a preposition, sometimes part of a more complex phrase, are also characteristic of formal writing, e.g.

- The ancient technique of 'stained glass', **in which** pigments were fired directly onto the surface of clear glass, has been updated recently.
- Bacteria and their products have been used extensively to control pests such as caterpillars, bollworms, corn borers, and fruit leaf rollers, **all of which** can damage crops used for food.
- The UK manufactures 750,000 tonnes of flat glass each year, **three quarters of which** goes into glazing products for buildings.

Practice (ii)

Add the correct preposition to the sentences:

at; of; above; in

1) There are several theories, most ____ which have been discussed at length in the literature.
2) This is the paper ____ which Maxwell's equations first appeared.
3) The line on the graph indicates the threshold ____ which the reaction is deemed significant.
4) Note the rate ____ which the solution heats up.
5) The plants produced pods, some ____ which were green, and some ____ which were yellow.

In possessive constructions, *whose* is commonly used with inanimate objects in academic writing: Biber *et al.* (1999: 618) found that 75% of *whose* in academic writing referred back to inanimate nouns, e.g.

They realised that only another planet, **whose** orbit lay beyond those already recognised, could explain the behaviour of the nearer planets.

These constructions can also be written as more complex phrases. Compare:

the orbit of which lay beyond those already recognised

Practice (iii)

Join these sentences together to form a single sentence containing a relative clause.

1) Arsenic is an extremely toxic substance. It is sometimes used as an insecticide.

   Arsenic _____

2) The Royal Society was founded in 1660. It is a self-governing fellowship of many of the world's most distinguished scientists.

   The Royal Society _____

3) The disease has a number of symptoms. Most of them can be controlled through medication.

   The disease _____

4) Technology can help countries to develop. It is unclear to what extent.

   The extent _____

5) Gravitational wave astronomy is an emerging new field of astronomy. It aims to use gravitational wave detectors to collect observational data about compact objects.

   Gravitational wave astronomy _____

6) A crystal is a piece of matter. Its boundaries are naturally formed plane surfaces.

   A crystal _____

7) Tim Berners-Lee invented the Internet. It was in 1989.

   It was Tim Berners-Lee _____

8) Fracking is a procedure. A solution is pumped into the earth to fracture rock and access oil and gas.

   Fracking _____

Think about how you could use this technique to produce a simple **paraphrase** of original sources. ▶ **Chapter 7**

Sentence structure 2

In this chapter you will look at different ways of combining elements in a sentence. You will also focus on an area which is often neglected, but which can greatly enhance the clarity and style of your writing: **punctuation**.

5.1 Combining ideas

In **Chapter 4**, you looked at how clauses combine in sentences. In this chapter, you will look at how words and phrases can be used to add meaning to clauses, and to link ideas and sentences together.

Explorative Task

*Which of the underlined parts of the sentences is **not** a clause (i.e. a **subject** + **verb** structure ▶ 4.1)?*

1) The drug was banned <u>because there were serious adverse side effects</u>.
2) The drug was banned <u>because of the serious adverse side effects</u>.
3) The drug had serious adverse side effects. <u>Because of the seriousness of these side effects</u>, the drug was banned.
4) The drug had serious adverse side effects. <u>Because of this</u>, it was banned.
5) The drug had serious adverse side effects. <u>Consequently</u>, it was banned.
6) The drug had serious side effects. <u>As a result</u>, it was banned.

> In 1), the underlined part of the sentence is a subordinate clause (▶ **4.2.2**). The underlined parts of 2), 3) and 4) are **prepositional phrases**, i.e. a preposition, *because of*, followed by a noun phrase (▶ **Appendix 2** on noun phrases). In sentence 5), *consequently* is an **adverb**. In sentence 6), *as a result* is also a **prepositional phrase**. Both 5) and 6) function as **sentence connectors**. All the underlined parts are **adverbials**, used to add information about the situation (▶ **4.2.1**).

5.1.1 Prepositional phrases

A prepositional phrase (preposition + noun) can occur in different positions, e.g.

- Unusual climatic events have occurred **throughout the year**.
- **Thanks to government funding**, the research is able to continue.

Some common examples of prepositions used in this way in academic writing are:

- Indicating time, duration or sequence: *in; on; during; throughout; since; until; before; after; prior to*
- Adding information: *in addition to; as well as*
- Indicating exception: *except for; apart from*
- Indicating cause: *because of; as a result of; due to; owing to; thanks to; on account of*
- Indicating concession: *despite; in spite of; notwithstanding*
- Introducing a focus: *with regard to; in terms of*
- Comparing and contrasting: *in comparison with; in contrast to*
- Specifying: *with regard to; with respect to*

Practice

Choose the correct preposition.

1) **In spite of/As a result of** measures introduced by the government to limit fuel emissions, pollution has continued to increase.
2) The patients in the study received chemotherapy **in addition to/because of** surgery.
3) **In addition to/Owing to** the risks involved, construction of the tunnel was abandoned.
4) Technology advanced rapidly **throughout/since** the industrial revolution.
5) The government agreed to fund the project, **notwithstanding/apart from** objections put forward by a number of renowned scientists.

5.1.2 Sentence connectors

Adverbs such as *however* and phrases such as *in addition* are often used at the beginning of a sentence to make a connection with the previous sentence. They can also sometimes appear in different positions (note the use of commas), e.g.

- However, the outcome was not positive for all patients.

- The outcome was not positive for all patients, however.
- The outcome was not, however, positive for all patients.

Some common examples of sentence connectors used in academic writing are:

- Sequencing: *firstly; secondly; finally; to begin with; subsequently*
- Adding information: *also; in addition; furthermore; moreover*
- Indicating result: *therefore; consequently; as a result; hence; thus*
- Comparing and contrasting: *similarly; in contrast*
- Indicating concession: *however; nevertheless; nonetheless*
- Emphasising: *in fact; above all; on the contrary*
- Rephrasing: *in other words; that is to say*

> Note that the adverbs *thereby*, *thus*, and *hence* can be followed by a complete sentence or be added to a main clause and followed by _____*ing*, e.g.
>
> The tribe employ a range of preserving techniques. Thus, they reduce food waste.
>
> The tribe employ a range of preserving techniques, **thus** reduc**ing** food waste.

Practice

Choose the correct expression.

1) The use of antibiotics in farming is increasing. **Consequently/Moreover**, resistance in the general population is decreasing.
2) The health service in the UK is funded through taxation. **On the contrary/In contrast**, the health service in the USA is based on private insurance.
3) Flood defences were constructed throughout the region. **However/Therefore**, many parts of the river broke through to flood the land.
4) Several buildings failed to withstand the earthquake. **In addition/Subsequently**, new building regulations were introduced.
5) Their data does not support current theories on rising sea levels. **Hence/On the contrary**, it seriously challenges them.

5.1.3 Controlling syntax

In this section, you will study and practise forming the different syntactic structures associated with conjunctions, prepositions and sentence connectors.

Practice (i)

*Decide which of these are **not** acceptable.*

1)
   a) There is a huge amount of soil erosion in the area as a result of the high rainfall.
   b) There is a huge amount of soil erosion in the area. As a result of the high rainfall.

   c) Rainfall is high in this area. As a result of this, there is a huge amount of soil erosion.
   d) Rainfall is high in this area. As a result, there is a huge amount of soil erosion.

2)
   a) In addition to their many useful built-in functions, smart phones run copious apps.
   b) In addition to having many useful built-in functions, smart phones run copious apps.
   c) Smart phones have many useful built-in functions. In addition, they run copious apps.
   d) In addition their many useful built-in functions, smart phones run copious apps.

3)
   a) The drug was banned because of its serious adverse side effects.
   b) The drug was banned because its serious side effects.
   c) The drug had serious adverse side effects. Because of this, it was banned.
   d) The drug was banned because there were serious adverse side effects.
   e) The drug was banned. Because it had serious side effects.

4)
   a) Asbestos is still widely used in some countries, despite of the serious health risk.
   b) Asbestos is still widely used in some countries in spite of/despite the serious health risk.
   c) Asbestos is still widely used in some countries in spite of/despite being a serious health risk.
   d) Asbestos is a serious health risk. In spite of/Despite this, it is still widely used in some countries.
   e) Asbestos is still widely used in some countries in spite of/despite the fact that there is a serious health risk.
   f) Asbestos is still widely used in some countries in spite of/despite there is a serious health risk.

Practice (ii)

Rewrite the sentences using the expressions given.

1) After studying computer science for a number of years, he did a PhD in software design.
   subsequently (sentence connector)
   He studied _____

2) It has been difficult for women to break into the field of science. Despite this, they have been responsible for many important discoveries.
   although (subordinating conjunction)
   Although _____

3) Although the water subsided quickly after the flood, there was still a huge amount of damage.
   however (sentence connector)
   The water _____

4) The patient was unable to sleep because he was stressed.
   due to (preposition)
   The patient _____

5) Plastics are widely used because they are very versatile. In addition, they are extremely durable.
   in addition to (preposition)
   In addition to _____

6) Some antibacterial products kill bacteria; others only prevent them from multiplying.
   while (conjunction)
   While _____

7) This model of phone is very popular. It has a high degree of functionality.
   owing to (preposition)
   This model of phone _____

Think about how you could use this technique to produce a simple **paraphrase** of
original sources. ▶ **Chapter 7**

Practice (iii)

Join the sentences in as many ways as you can, using the expressions given.

1) The treatment has a high success rate. It has not been adopted on a wide scale.
   despite/in spite of

   _____

   _____

   _____

2) Huge areas of rain forest are being destroyed every day. The number of animal species
   found in these regions is declining.
   result/because

   _____

   _____

   _____

3) Dyes have many industrial applications. They are also widely used in medicine.
   addition

   _____

   _____

   _____

5.2 Focus on punctuation

Punctuation in English can be viewed as stylistic or grammatical.

Stylistic punctuation can involve, for example, deciding between a full stop or a semi-
colon between two sentences. People have different preferences, and acceptable variation
can be found across academic texts. However, these choices are still important because
they can affect clarity and readability.

Grammatical punctuation is not a matter of choice because the punctuation here is intrinsically connected to the meaning, as we saw with relative clauses in **4.2.4**.

Focussing on punctuation can help you to consolidate your understanding of sentence structure as a whole.

Good command of punctuation can help you achieve clarity and focus in your writing.

Explorative Task

*Which of the pairs do you find easier to read or more effective? Why? Compare your ideas with the **Study Box** which follows.*

1)
    a)   In 1929 Alexander Fleming discovered penicillin.
    b)   In 1929, Alexander Fleming discovered penicillin.

2)
    a)   St Thomas' hospital concerned about the number of infections began to transfer patients to other centres.
    b)   St Thomas' hospital, concerned about the number of infections, began to transfer patients to other centres.

3)
    a)   Newton the great mathematician and physicist formulated three laws of motion.
    b)   Newton, the great mathematician and physicist, formulated three laws of motion.

4)
    a)   The guidelines concerning the prevention of type 2 diabetes recommend plenty of exercise and they propose a diet based around protein, slow-release carbohydrates and fruit and vegetables.
    b)   The guidelines concerning the prevention of type 2 diabetes recommend plenty of exercise, and they propose a diet based around protein, slow-release carbohydrates, and fruit and vegetables.

5)
    a)   If detected early enough the disease is treatable.
    b)   If detected early enough, the disease is treatable.

6)
    a)   The disease is treatable if detected early enough.
    b)   The disease is treatable, if detected early enough.

7)
    a)   Aristotle believed the world to be composed of four elements, earth, water, air and fire.
    b)   Aristotle believed the world to be composed of four elements: earth, water, air and fire.

8)
    a)   Mammals are warm-blooded. Reptiles are cold-blooded.
    b)   Mammals are warm-blooded; reptiles are cold-blooded.

Study Box: Common punctuation patterns

Examples taken from:

Dawkins, R. (ed.) (2008) *The Oxford Book of Modern Science Writing*.

Commas

> Commas are the equivalent of changing gear when driving; you come to a point where you need to slow down a little or turn a corner. The commas help you negotiate these changes, but also, and perhaps more importantly, they enable you to take your reader along with you.
>
> Peck and Coyle (2012: 54)

Think of commas, therefore, as a way to guide (or drive!) your reader through the text.

1) It can make a sentence easier to follow for the reader if you separate words and phrases coming before (or sometimes after) a clause with a comma (see 1 above), especially in longer sentences, e.g.

> From Pythagoras to string theory, the desire to comprehend nature has been framed by the Platonic ideal that the world is a reflection of some perfect mathematical form.

The comma serves to 'introduce' the main point, thus guiding the reader.

Likewise, use commas if a word or phrase 'interrupts' a clause or structure (see 2 above), e.g.

> It is mathematics, more than anything else, that is responsible for the obscurity that surrounds the creative process of theoretical physics.

In this way, the reader is able to extract the main point easily.

This principle applies to phrases used in 'apposition' (i.e. consecutive phrases, usually noun phrases, the second one defining or modifying the first – see 3 above), e.g.

> Aristotle, the first great biologist, wrote that each sense organ 'receives the form of the other object without its matter'.

2) It is optional to use a comma before *and/but/or* to separate coordinate clauses (▶ **4.2.2.1**), but it can often help to make long sentences easier to read (see 4 above); when listing items, a comma can also help avoid confusion (see 4 above), e.g.

> Parallel advances in biochemistry have provided us with detailed knowledge of how energy is converted to chemical bonds and chemical bonds to energy, and how the elementary components of living cells are synthesised.

3) Separate the main clause and subordinate clause with a comma when the subordinate clause comes first (see 5 above) (▶ **4.2.2.2**), e.g.

> If we examine the process of DNA replication, we see that there are a number of basic requirements.

continued . . .

cont.

If the main clause comes first, it is not necessary to use a comma, although people often do, and it is considered acceptable if it makes sense. (In 6 above, the comma is unnecessary, but could be used to add emphasis; however, in general, avoid commas which are unnecessary as they can make the page too 'busy' and difficult to read – like driving along a bumpy road!)

4) Use commas to separate non-defining relative clauses from the main clause (▶ **4.2.4**), e.g.

   Darwin regarded his work as a clear break with past biology, which believed in an instantaneous creation of an unchanging world whose various parts functioned together like so many parts of a clock.

5) Do not use commas:

   in defining/restrictive relative clauses (▶ **4.2.4**), e.g.

   This is the first book, that/which he wrote. ✗

   to introduce *that*-clauses (▶ **4.2.3.2**), e.g.

   It is thought, that these climatic events will continue. ✗

   directly in between a subject and verb, no matter how long the subject (▶ **Appendix 2**), e.g.

   The most significant discoveries made in this period, were in the field of space exploration. ✗

Colons and Semi-colons

1) Use a colon to introduce a sentence that expands in some way on the previous one, by, for example, providing an explanation, or listing items (see 7 above), e.g.

   The graph of points for pairs of snapping shrimps always shows a correlation of the sizes of mates: bigger males pair with bigger females, smaller males with smaller females.

   ▶ **9.1** for information on using colons in referencing
   ▶ **9.2** for information on using colons in quotations

2) A semi-colon can be used instead of a full stop to separate sentences which are closely connected (see 8 above), e.g.

   A newborn infant is not a blank page; however, his genes do not seal his fate.

   Atoms are assembled into complex molecules; these react, via complex pathways in every cell, and indirectly lead to the entire interconnected structure that makes up a tree, an insect or a human.

   ▶ **5.3** for information on commas, colons and semi-colons in **lists**
   ▶ **9.1 Appendix 3** for information on apostrophes, hyphens etc.

Practice

Add commas, colons or semi-colons to the following sentences where necessary or so that they are easier to follow. Note that some sentences do not require any further punctuation, i.e. it would make them grammatically incorrect.

1) Over the past two centuries pollution has become one of the most pervasive and multi-faceted threats to human health.

2) In 1988 the Centers for Disease Control (CDC) concerned about the spread of HIV in hospitals published a set of universal procedures requiring all medical facilities in the United States to conform to specific guidelines for patient care (Table 6.2).

3) Darwin was concerned with evolution i.e. change over time and he proposed a process natural selection that could bring about such change.

4) Chemical reactions normally occur in water and water can also participate in reactions.

5) If every individual in the world were to demand as much energy as the average person uses in North America the global energy supply industries would require a five-fold increase in their use of primary energy sources.

6) After felling a tree has to be processed in order to render the timber suitable for man's use.

7) The calculus of variations which plays an important role in both pure and applied mathematics dates from the time of Newton.

8) The computers which form the basis of those used today were mainly developed in the 1940s.

9) Scientists are able to identify parts of the brain that are specifically targeted by addictive drugs.

10) Einstein in his general theory of relativity (1915) proposed that the universe exists in four-dimensional space-time.

11) Aromatherapy users showed prominent characteristics they were far more likely to be younger females highly educated who tend to live in urban areas.

12) The pH of the heartwood varies in different species of timber but is generally about 4.5 to 5.5 however in some timbers such as eucalypt oak and western red cedar the pH of the heartwood can be as low as 3.0.

5.3 Lists and parallel structures

When two or more similar things are mentioned in a sentence, **parallel structures**, that is to say repetition of words, phrases and syntactic patterns (including punctuation), are often employed.

Multiple items are also often presented as **lists**. Items in a list should be balanced in terms of grammatical structure, i.e. they should be parallel structures.

These two devices, lists and parallel structures, when carefully constructed and punctuated, can greatly improve clarity and readability.

Explorative Task

*Find examples of lists and parallel structures in the sentences below. What do you notice about punctuation? Compare your ideas to the features listed in the **Study Box** that follows.*

1) Some of the most unusual and versatile of all the mammals are the groups that live, feed and reproduce under water.
2) Epidemic outbreaks of disease are fostered by factors such as poor socioeconomic conditions, ignorance of the cause of infection, natural disasters, and poor hygiene.
3) In actively respiring tissues, where the concentration of carbon dioxide is high, haemoglobin readily releases its oxygen, while in the lungs, where blood carbon dioxide is low, haemoglobin readily binds oxygen.
4) A cancer that arises in epithelium is called a carcinoma; one that arises in connective tissue is called a sarcoma.
5) There are three basic types of water pollutants: toxic chemicals, biological materials and thermal discharges.
6) Optical astronomical telescopes fall into two main classes: refracting telescopes (or refractors), which use lenses to form the primary image, and reflecting telescopes (or reflectors), which use mirrors.
7) The cell cycle can be divided into four main stages: the M phase, which consists of mitosis (nuclear division) and cytokinesis (cytoplasmic division); the G_1 phase, in which there is a high rate of biosynthesis and growth; the S phase, in which the DNA content of the cell doubles and the chromosomes replicate; the G_2 phase, during which the final preparations for cell division are made.

Study Box: Punctuation in lists and parallel structures

1) Three simple items in a list should be written *a, b and c*, though a comma is often used before *and*, and can sometimes aid clarity if the items are long or contain another *and* within, e.g.

   an equal balance of carbohydrates, fruit and vegetables, and protein

2) Precise, 'mirrored' (i.e. the same punctuation used in each parallel item), use of commas can enhance the use of parallel structures and improve readability.
3) Semi-colons can also be used to enhance the link between parallel structures.
4) A colon can be used to introduce a list, especially if it is complex. The items in a list can be separated with commas if fairly short and simple; longer, more complex items should be separated by semi-colons. As you can see from 7, this type of structure can be extended to form a whole, single-sentence paragraph.

continued . . .

cont.

▶ **Chapter 9.7** for information on more detailed lists

Be careful to avoid 'false parallelism', i.e. when items in a list do not share the same grammar, e.g.

Composite materials are widely used in a variety of applications in, for example, transport, construction, and biomedical. ✗

Composite materials are widely used in a variety of applications in, for example, transport, construction and **biomedicine**. ✓

Practice

Combine the notes below to form sentences. Use parallel structures where possible, and commas, colons and semi-colons where necessary. You will also need to form the verb correctly, add articles, etc., in order to form grammatical sentences.

1) rock – three types – igneous/sedimentary/metamorphic

2) blood vessels – three types – arteries (carry blood away from heart)/capillaries (connect arteries to veins)/veins (carry blood back to heart)

3) deciduous trees (lose their leaves seasonally)/evergreen trees (green foliage all year round)

4) taste – four types (according to western experts) – sweet/salty/sour/bitter – also umami (according to eastern experts)

5) trunk of a tree – three physical functions to perform – firstly must support crown – region responsible for production of food and seed – secondly must conduct mineral solutions absorbed by roots upwards to crown – thirdly must store manufactured food (carbohydrates) until required

6 Paragraph development: achieving flow

In this chapter, you will examine some of the characteristics of typical English paragraph structure, and learn how to develop your own paragraphs in a clear way.

A paragraph is well developed if there is a logical connection between ideas, and the words, sentences and ideas **flow** in such a way that the reader is able to follow easily.

Explorative Task

Which of the student's two drafts below is easier to read? Why?

Text A

The dithiocarbamate drug disulfiram is used in the treatment of alcohol abuse. The drug induces apoptosis* in cancer tumours. It has recently been discovered that disulfiram has potential therapeutic capabilities.[1] It has been reported that disulfiram in combination with copper (II) salts causes apoptosis in a chemotherapy-resistant cancer cell line.[2] The copper complex of the drug enhances the result against the tumour cells.
*cell death

Text B

The dithiocarbamate drug disulfiram is primarily used in the treatment of alcohol abuse. Recently, however, other potential therapeutic capabilities have been discovered.[1] It has been reported that disulfiram causes apoptosis in a chemotherapy-resistant cancer cell line. This effect is enhanced if the drug is used in combination with copper (II) salts.[2]

> Text A is the student's first draft. Although accurate and well-expressed on the whole, it is a little hard to follow because some information is repeated at different points and it is not as concise as it could be. Text B is the student's second draft. It flows clearly and concisely from point to point, and uses certain expressions (*primarily/ other; however; this effect*) to make logical connections.

Things which contribute to flow are:

- **information structure**
- **cohesive devices**
- **punctuation**

These will be discussed in the following sections.

6.1 Information structure

One thing which can aid flow is the structuring of information in a clear, logical way. Information structure can differ across languages, so there are some specific things about English information structure which you need to be aware of.

6.1.1 Given versus new information

The order of information can contribute significantly to how a text flows.

Explorative Task

1) *Look at the paragraphs below and decide which one is easiest to read.*

(i)

Text A

Food additives are substances that are added to food to improve shelf-life, appearance and flavour. Vinegar and salt are two substances which have been added to food for centuries. Modern food processing has led to the use of many more additives, both natural and artificial.

Text B

Food additives are substances that are added to food to improve shelf-life, appearance and flavour. Two substances which have been added to food for centuries are vinegar and salt. Many more additives, both natural and artificial, are now used in modern food processing.

(ii)

Text A

Geckos, harmless tropical lizards, are extremely fascinating and extraordinary animals. They have very sticky feet that cling to virtually any surface. This characteristic makes it possible for them to rapidly run up vertical walls and along the undersides of horizontal surfaces. In fact, a gecko can support its body mass with a single toe! The secret to this remarkable ability is the presence of an extremely large number of microscopically small hairs on each of their toe pads. When these hairs come into contact with a surface, weak forces of attraction (i.e. van der Waals forces) are established between hair molecules and molecules on the surface. The fact that these hairs are so small and so numerous explains why the gecko grips surfaces so tightly. To release its grip, the gecko simply curls up its toes, and peels the hairs away from the surface.

Text B

Geckos, harmless tropical lizards, are extremely fascinating and extraordinary animals. They have very sticky feet that cling to virtually any surface. They are able to rapidly run up vertical walls and along the undersides of horizontal surfaces, thanks to this characteristic. In fact, a gecko can support its body mass with a single toe! The presence of an extremely large number of microscopically small hairs on each of their toe pads is the secret to this remarkable ability. Weak forces of attraction (i.e. van der Waals forces) are established between hair molecules and molecules on the surface when these hairs come into contact with a surface. The fact that these hairs are so small and so numerous explains why the gecko grips surfaces so tightly. The gecko simply curls up its toes, and peels the hairs away from the surface to release its grip.

Texts 1 B (adapted from *The Royal Society*) and 2 A (Callister, 2007: 15) are the original texts. Both have a typical English information structure in that each sentence first refers back to the main theme of the previous sentence and then adds new information. This maintains the flow of information. (In contrast, in 1 A and 2 B, the link to what has gone before is delayed, making it difficult to follow.)

This **given → new** structure also allows for another common feature of English, **end focus**, whereby new information comes at the end of the sentence, where it has more prominence.

2) *Look back at the texts 1 B and 2 A and underline the words/phrases which link back to information already given.* *(The use of such links is examined further in 6.2.)*

Practice

*Rewrite these short texts to reflect the **given** → **new** structure exemplified above.*

1) Cereals are one of the most important staple foods. Wheat, rye, barley, oats, maize, rice, millet and sorghum are the major cereals of the world.

    _____

    _____

2) Beer is a fermented alcoholic beverage. Malt and hops are the main ingredients of beer.

    _____

    _____

3) A ligament is a resilient but flexible band of tissue that holds two or more bones together at a moveable joint. Movement of bones at a joint is restrained by ligaments and therefore they are important in preventing dislocation.

    _____

    _____

4) Chalk is a very fine-grained white rock composed of the fossilised skeletal remains of marine plankton and consisting largely of calcium carbonate. Toothpaste and cosmetics use chalk. However, blackboard 'chalk' is not the same thing. It is made from calcium sulphate.

    _____

    _____

6.1.2 General and specific

Sentences in a paragraph must be logically ordered, and often follow a linear **general** → **specific** pattern. It is also common to make the first sentence a sort of general 'umbrella' (i.e. covering the rest of the paragraph) statement, which introduces the main theme of the paragraph: this is often referred to as the **topic sentence**. Subsequent sentences will expand in some way on this, by providing support such as explanation or exemplification.

Explorative Task

*Look at how the paragraphs below are introduced and developed, and match each sentence with a description of its function in the paragraph, making particular note of the **topic sentence** in each.*

    Text A

    Infectious diseases remain a major threat to global animal and human health. Recent examples include the 2002 Foot and Mouth Disease outbreak in the UK, the 2003 global epidemic of SARS and the threat of an influenza pandemic. The control of infectious diseases in animals and humans is a problem that needs to be addressed by scientists, veterinarians, healthcare workers, economists, social scientists and policy makers.

(Adapted from *The Royal society*)

sentence 1	a) **gives** examples
sentence 2	b) **introduces** the threat of infectious diseases
sentence 3	c) **states** the need for problem to be addressed

Text B

Unless a patient needing an organ has an identical twin, there will always be immunological differences between the patient and the transplanted organ. These differences are immediately recognised by the recipient's immune system, and, depending on how closely the donor and recipient were matched, cause a reaction intended to destroy the transplanted organ. Consequently, transplant patients are placed on drug regimens designed to lessen the immune response against the organ to prevent rejection. These drugs reduce the chances of rejection by diminishing the patients' *overall* immune capability. However, this causes the patient to be more susceptible to infection.

(Strelkauskas *et al.*, 2010: 106)

sentence 1	a) **states** the problem
sentence 2	b) **explains** the negative side effects of the drugs
sentence 3	c) **introduces** the current solution to the problem (drugs)
sentence 4	d) **explains** how the drugs work
sentence 5	e) **introduces** the issue of immunological differences in organ transplant patients

Text C

The *Capsicum* family includes a wide variety of peppers ranging from the large sweet peppers to the fiery chilli peppers. Chilli peppers derive their hotness from capsaicin and dihydrocapsaicin (members of the capsaicinoid family), and restaurants specializing in 'hot' foods owe much to these molecules of nature. They work by interacting with the same receptors in your mouth that sense heat. Excessive amounts of capsaicin are toxic because capsaicin prevents the production of certain neurotransmitters and affects the function of neuroproteins in the brain. At high enough concentrations, capsaicin destroys 'substance P' in the nervous system. This effect has now been harnessed for medical use: 'substance P' is associated with the pain suffered by people with, for example, arthritis and inflammatory bowel disease, and application of a cream containing capsaicin results in pain relief.

(Housecroft and Constable, 2010: 1215)

sentence 1	a) **explains** the source of chilli heat
sentence 2	b) **introduces** the capsicum family
sentence 3	c) **explains** the toxic nature of one 'heat' molecule – capsaicin
sentence 4	d) **gives** examples of medical uses of capsaicin
sentence 5	e) **explains** the effects of capsaicin
sentence 6	f) **explains** how the 'heat' molecules produce heat

Note the verbs in bold (*introduce; state; give; explain*), which show that each sentence has a clear role, or function in the paragraph. For example, it can be clearly seen from the above texts that the role of the **topic sentence** is usually to **introduce** the main theme of the text. Think about what you want each sentence to **do** in your text.

Practice

Put the sentences below in order to form well-developed paragraphs. Take care to identify the

topic sentence.

Text A

1) _____ 2) _____ 3) _____ 4) _____ 5) _____

a) More efficient fluorescent lighting has since been developed, but suffers from flicker and colour purity issues.
b) They are already used in traffic lights and even in museums to illuminate paintings.
c) Lighting has not changed much since the light bulb was invented by Edison and others close to a hundred years ago.
d) LEDs exhibit tremendous brightness, consume little power, come in different colors, and emit little or no heat.
e) Recently, solid state light-emitting diodes (LEDs) have come on the market and are poised to revolutionise the lighting industry.

(Kuno, 2012: 419–420)

Text B

1) _____ 2) _____ 3) _____ 4) _____ 5) _____ 6) _____ 7) _____ 8) _____

a) 'Triggers' external to the climate system, such as changes in the Earth's orbit or a brightening or dimming of the sun, could bring this about; so could internal triggers such as emissions of climate-altering gases into the atmosphere.

b) However, palaeoclimatic records show that large, abrupt changes to the global climate have occurred frequently.

c) Temperature changes of up to 16 degrees Celsius and precipitation doublings, for example, have occurred in periods as short as decades or less (Committee on Abrupt Climate Change, National Research Council, 2002) and might therefore presumably happen again.

d) The majority of climate scientists believe the world is in a period of climate warning and associated environmental change and that this is likely to continue for a long time, with significant impacts on human health around the globe.

e) Projected changes this century, while alarming, are envisaged as relatively gradual, making adaptation to the changes easier than would be the case with larger and more abrupt change.

f) Such changes occur when a threshold in the climate system is crossed.

g) This would clearly have enormous impacts on global health futures.

h) This raises the question of whether human-induced greenhouse gas emissions might ultimately trigger abrupt, larger climate change than is currently predicted.

(McCracken and Phillips, 2012: 287–288)

6.2 Cohesive devices

There should be logical connections between the ideas in a paragraph. These logical connections can be indicated through the organisation and grammar of the text, and sometimes by the use of particular words and phrases. Look back at the paragraphs you formed in **6.1.2** on lighting and climate change.

How were you able to make logical connections between the sentences?

Did the grammar or particular words/phrases help you to link the sentences/ideas together?

You should notice that there are many ways to indicate logical connections in a text; it is not just a case of adding lots of 'linking words' like *however* (although these can help if used with care and precision).

Explorative Task

1) *Look again at the texts from* **6.1.2** *repeated below. This time, some examples of cohesion have been highlighted. Consider how these words/phrases help you to make logical connections between the ideas. Find examples of:*

- *the use of repetition and synonyms*
- *the use of pronouns and other expressions to refer back to what has been said*
- *the use of linking expressions*

Text A

Infectious diseases remain a major threat to global animal and human health. **Recent examples** (1) include the 2002 Foot and Mouth Disease outbreak in the UK, the 2003 global epidemic of SARS and the threat of an influenza pandemic. The control of **infectious diseases** (2) in animals and humans is a problem that needs to be addressed by scientists, veterinarians, healthcare workers, economists, social scientists and policy makers.

Text B

Unless a patient needing an organ has an identical twin, there will always be immunological differences between the patient and the transplanted organ. **These differences** (3) are immediately recognised by the recipient's immune system, and, depending on how closely the donor and recipient were matched, cause a reaction intended to destroy the transplanted organ. **Consequently** (4), transplant patients are placed on drug regimens designed to lessen the immune response against the organ to prevent rejection. **These drugs** (5) reduce the chances of rejection by diminishing the patients' *overall* immune capability. **However** (6), this causes the patient to be more susceptible to infection.

Text C

The *Capsicum* family includes a wide variety of peppers ranging from the large sweet peppers to the **fiery** (7) chilli peppers. Chilli peppers derive **their** (8) **hotness** (9) from capsaicin and dihydrocapsaicin (members of the capsaicinoid family), and restaurants specializing in '**hot**' (10) foods owe much to **these molecules of nature** (11). **They** (12) work by interacting with the same receptors in your mouth **that** (13) sense **heat** (14). Excessive amounts of **capsaicin** (15) are toxic because **capsaicin** (16) prevents the production of certain neurotransmitters and affects the function of neuroproteins in the brain. At high enough concentrations, **capsaicin** (17) destroys 'substance P' in the nervous system. **This effect** (18) has now been harnessed for medical use: 'substance P' is associated with the pain suffered by people with, for example, arthritis and inflammatory bowel disease, and application of a cream containing **capsaicin** (19) results in pain relief.

The paragraphs above use a range of cohesive devices to link ideas together. These are listed below with examples from the texts:

1) repetition of words and phrases: (2) (15) (16) (17) (19)
2) the use of synonyms: (7) and (10); (9) and (14)
3) the use of 'ellipsis', i.e. when words are left out because they are understood through what has gone before (1)
4) the use of pronouns, including relative pronouns (▶ **4.2.4**), to refer back to nouns (8) (12) (13)
5) the use of *this/these* + noun (occasionally *that/those*) to refer back to nouns (3) (5) (11) (18)
6) the use of linking words/phrases (4) (6)

2) Add more examples to the list above from the paragraph below.

The body can defend itself against infection by using two types of immune response, **the innate** (20) and **the adaptive** (21). **The innate immune response** (22) is available to us when we are born and is nonspecific, where nonspecific means that **this response** (23) can react against any infection or pathogen. **In contrast** (24), **the adaptive immune response** (25) is specific, meaning that it responds against a specific pathogen. **The adaptive immune response** (26) also has the gift of 'memory', **which** (27) allows **it** (28) to remember any pathogen **it** (29) reacted against in the past and to respond quickly and powerfully if **that pathogen** (30) returns.

(Strelkauskas *et al.*, 2010: 325)

Study Box: Ways to improve cohesion

1) When you refer back to a noun mentioned earlier in the text, consider whether you should use a pronoun, for example *it/them*, or whether you need to repeat the word to avoid vagueness or ambiguity. Do not be afraid of some repetition as it often aids clarity and can be used elegantly (▶ **5.3** on **parallel structures**); this is not the same as redundancy, where words are repeated through a lack of conciseness, or information is repeated because the text does not have a clear, linear structure.
2) If you decide to use a synonym, make sure it really is a synonym!
3) When you refer back to something earlier in the text, think about whether you should use a singular or plural pronoun, e.g. *it* or *them/this* or *these*.
4) Use linking words carefully and precisely to add real meaning; do not use them as decoration!

Practice (i)

Complete the text, by choosing from the pronouns below, so that it is grammatical and makes sense:

it/its
this/that/which

One of the most energetic explosive events known is a supernova. These occur at the end of a star's lifetime, when (1) _____ nuclear fuel is exhausted and (2) _____ is no longer supported by the release of nuclear energy. If the star is particularly massive, then (3) _____ core will collapse and in so doing will release a huge amount of energy. (4) _____ will cause a blast wave (5) _____ ejects the star's envelope into interstellar space. The result of the collapse may be, in some cases, a rapidly rotating neutron star that can be observed many years later as a radio pulsar.
(High Energy Astrophysics Science Archive Research Centre, *Supernova*)

Practice (ii)

Select the best option to complete the text so that it flows easily.

Taking omega-3 fish oils could help to protect against skin cancer, Manchester researchers have found. (1) **The researchers/They** analysed the effect of taking (2) **omega-3/it** on healthy volunteers and found a regular dose boosted skin immunity to sunlight. (3) **Omega-3/It** also reduced sunlight-induced suppression of the immune system, (4) **it/which** affects the body's ability to fight skin cancer and infection.

Professor Lesley Rhodes, from the Photobiology Unit Dermatology Centre, based at the School of Medicine and Salford Royal NHS Foundation Trust, said: 'Although the changes we found when someone took the oil were small, (5) **it/they** suggest that a continuous low level of chemoprevention from taking (6) **omega-3/it** could reduce the risk of cancer over an individual's lifetime.'

(7) **Professor Lesley Rhodes/She** added that (8) **omega-3/it** was not a substitute for sunscreen and physical protection, but should be regarded as an additional small measure to help protect skin from sun damage.

(Unilife, 2013: 10)

Practice (iii)

Complete the text with a word or phrase from below so that the connections between ideas are clear:

thus; this knowledge; furthermore; for example; these new materials; these; at this point

The earliest humans had access to only a very limited number of materials, those that occur naturally: stone, wood, clay, skins and so on. With time they discovered techniques for producing materials that had properties superior to those of the natural ones; (1) _____ included pottery and various metals. (2) _____, it was discovered that the properties of a material could be altered by heat treatments and by the addition of other substances. (3) _____, materials utilization was totally a selection process that involved deciding from a given, rather limited set of materials the one best suited for an application by virtue of its characteristics. It was not until relatively recent times that scientists came to understand the relationships between the structural elements of materials and their properties. (4) _____, acquired over approximately the past hundred years, has empowered them to fashion, to a large degree, the characteristics of the materials. (5) _____, tens of thousands of different materials have evolved with rather specialized characteristics that meet the needs of our modern and complex society; (6) _____ include metals, plastics, glasses, and fibres.

The development of many technologies that make our existence so comfortable has been ultimately associated with the accessibility of suitable materials. An advancement in the understanding of a material type is often the forerunner to the stepwise progression of technology. (7) _____, automobiles would not have been possible without the availability of inexpensive steel or some other comparable substitute. In our contemporary era, sophisticated electronic devices rely on components for what are called semiconducting materials.

(Callister, 2007: 2)

6.3 Focus on punctuation

As you saw in **Chapters 4** and **5**, careful use of punctuation can add significantly to clarity of expression in sentences. It can also greatly improve the flow and readability of a paragraph.

Practice

Punctuate the following passage so that it flows and makes sense.

an animals survival prospects are greatly improved if the animal alters its behaviour according to its experience learning increases its chances of obtaining food avoiding predators and adjusting to other often unpredictable changes in its environment the importance of learning in the development of behaviour was stressed particularly by us experimental psychologists such as john b watson 1878–1958 and b f skinner 1904–90 who studied animals under carefully controlled laboratory conditions they demonstrated how rats and pigeons could be trained or conditioned by exposing them to stimuli in the form of food rewards or electric shocks this work was criticised by others notably ethologists who preferred to observe animals in their natural surroundings and who stressed the importance of inborn mechanisms such as instinct in behavioural development a synthesis between these two once conflicting approaches has been achieved learning is regarded as a vital aspect of an animals development occurring in response to stimuli in the animals environment but within the constraints set by the animals genes hence young animals are receptive to a wide range of stimuli but are genetically predisposed to respond to those that are more significant

(*Oxford Dictionary of Science*, 2005: 470)

Review Task

Combine the notes below to form clear, readable paragraphs. Consider:

- *information structure*
- *cohesive devices*
- *punctuation*

(Remember these are notes: you will need to 'add grammar' - articles, verb forms, etc., as well as linking together ideas.)

1) *Recycling*
   recycling products is better than disposing of them as waste - two main reasons:
   - less need to extract raw materials from the earth - conserves natural resources
   - energy requirements for refinement and processing of recycled materials usually less than for natural resources

▶ Model Text 5, Appendix 4

2) *Additives and chemicals*
   many foods contain chemical additives – e.g. preservatives; artificial sweeteners; artificial flavourings; colouring agents

   added by manufacturer – during production

   chemicals also enter food chain through agriculture:
   - widespread use of fertilisers and pesticides on crops
   - antibiotics and supplements for livestock

   maximum allowed levels strictly controlled by law – therefore quality control of raw materials and commercially manufactured foodstuffs essential to ensure they are not contaminated beyond regulatory levels

   one technique used: *high-performance liquid chromatography (HPLC)* (technique used to separate, identify and quantify components in a mixture) used in combination with a detection system, often *ultraviolet–visible (UV–VIS) spectroscopy*

▶ Model Text 6, Appendix 4

Referring to sources: paraphrase, refer-encing, criticality and the issue of plagiarism

When you complete a writing assignment, you will need to find out new things and to position yourself within your field of study. This involves making use of, and making reference to, the scholarly work of others, often authorities in your subject.

In this chapter, you will firstly reflect on your own views on using the work of others in your own writing.

You will then focus on the issue of **plagiarism**, considering what it really means to 'use your own words', and exploring the notion of **good academic practice** in relation to the use of sources.

The chapter will then present some strategies for **paraphrase** and **summary** which will help you to use academic sources in a positive way.

Finally, you will think about how to use your reading to build your own collection of useful structures and phrases to use in your writing as a whole.

░ **Explorative Task**

Consider these comments made by students. Are the students right or wrong? *The issues that arise will be discussed in the following sections.*

*   "If I have lots of references to other people's work, it won't be *my* work, it won't be original."
*   "I can use other people's words as long as I give a reference."
*   "If I use my own words to explain someone else's work, I don't need to give a reference.
*   "I can paraphrase by replacing some words with synonyms."
*   "I must change every word in a source I am using."

7.1 Using your own words

When referring to the work of others you might:

*   **paraphrase**, i.e. explain something with roughly the same amount of detail

*   **summarise**, i.e. convey the main ideas of a passage, chapter, article or book in fewer words

*   **quote**, i.e. use somebody else's exact words (relatively infrequent in scientific texts, though sometimes useful, especially for precise definitions): ▶ **9.2** for information on incorporating quotation into your writing

It is important to know which technique is appropriate. It is also important to make sure that the work you produce in this way reflects your own understanding and analysis of the subject and of the sources you have consulted.

7.1.1 The issue of plagiarism

Plagiarism is, rightly, an important issue in the academic world and beyond. It is basically 'academic theft' (of words or ideas), an unethical practice which can have very serious consequences.

Plagiarism can be intentional, i.e. when a student knowingly copies something and just hopes they will not get caught! But more often than not it arises because of a misunderstanding about what plagiarism is, and why it is such a bad thing in terms of academic practice.

The emphasis in this chapter is not on 'avoiding plagiarism', as this would place emphasis on the most obviously *negative* aspect of plagiarism, i.e. getting caught copying! Here, the aim is to make you think about the *positive* aspects of producing work which is not plagiarised.

7.1.2 Good reasons to use your own words

Explorative Task (i)

Think of three reasons why it is a good thing to use your own words when you include information or ideas from other sources:

1) _____
2) _____
3) _____

*Now compare your ideas with the advice in the **Study Box** below.*

Study Box: Good reasons to use your own words

1) Most obviously, using your own words is necessary in order to avoid plagiarism. (Most universities use *Turnitin* software to check for plagiarism.)
2) Using your own words is important, not simply because it enables you to avoid copying, but because it allows you to show that you understand what you have read and can explain it in a clear, concise way. The person reading and assessing your work cannot know if you understand a complex scientific concept if you merely reproduce someone else's explanation of it! What's more, as you struggle with the process of explaining difficult scientific concepts in your own words, you will get a good idea of just how well you understand them.
3) Using your own words gives you more scope to refer to sources **critically**, tying them in to your own ideas and argument, rather than just reproducing the thoughts of others. ▶ 7.2

Explorative Task (ii)

Look at the original text and the paraphrases, and then complete the table below.

Original text

Much of chemistry is concerned with chemical reactions. The factors that control whether a reaction will or will not take place fall into two categories: *thermodynamic* and *kinetic*. Thermodynamic concepts relate to the energetics of a system, while kinetics deal with the speed at which a reaction occurs. Observations of reaction kinetics are related to the mechanism of the reaction, and this describes the way in which we believe that the atoms and molecules behave during a reaction.
C. E. Housecroft and E. C. Constable, *Chemistry: An Introduction to Organic, Inorganic and Physical Chemistry*, (4th Edition), Harlow, Pearson Education, 2010, 339.

Paraphrase A

A great deal of chemistry is concerned with chemical reactions. The factors that control if a reaction will or will not take place fall into two classes: *thermodynamic* and *kinetic*. Thermodynamic ideas are related to the energetics of a system, whereas kinetics deal with the speed at which a reaction occurs. Observations of reaction kinetics relate to the reaction's mechanism, the way in which we think that the atoms and molecules behave during a reaction.

Paraphrase B

Chemical reactions, and the factors affecting them, are central to chemistry. Whether or not a reaction will occur is determined by *thermodynamics*, which relates to the energetics (the nature of energy in transformation) of a system, and *kinetics*, which relates to the speed of a reaction.

Paraphrase C

Chemical reactions, and the factors affecting them, are central to chemistry. Whether or not a reaction will occur is determined by *thermodynamics*, which relates to the energetics (the nature of energy in transformation) of a system, and *kinetics*, which relates to the speed of a reaction.[1]

References

1. C. E. Housecroft and E. C. Constable, *Chemistry: An Introduction to Organic, Inorganic and Physical Chemistry*, (4th Edition), Harlow, Pearson Education, 2010, 339.

Which text	Text A	Text B	Text C
uses different sentence structure and phrasing, just retaining technical terms?			
selects particular information?			
adds some information?			
is clearly referenced?			
is an acceptable paraphrase?			

Note that Paraphrase A has simply adopted a mechanical word-changing approach. B and C both explain the information they have selected in their own words (and add their own explanation where necessary), but B is still plagiarism, as there is no acknowledgement that the *facts*, if not the actual *words* have been taken from a textbook.

7.1.3 Good reasons *not* to use your own words

Explorative Task (i)

*Think of two instances when it is actually better **not** to use your own words:*

1) _____

2) _____

*Now compare your ideas with the advice in the **Study Box** below.*

Study Box: Good reasons *not* to use your own words

1) Positioning yourself within your own scientific discipline involves using a great deal of technical language common to everyone working within that discipline (e.g. *chemical reaction*). In fact, trying to change this language will lead to unnatural, unclear expression.

2) Occasionally, it will be useful to employ someone else's exact words, to give a precise definition of a difficult concept, for example. However, if you do this, you must clearly indicate that it is a quote by using speech marks (▶ 9.2 for information on incorporating quotation into your writing).

Also ...

3) It is clear that demonstrating understanding of the text you are paraphrasing necessarily involves using structures and phrasing **not** contained in that actual text. However, any text you are reading is likely to contain a range of fairly fixed structures and expressions which are used across academic writing. If you notice this language, make a note of it, and use it in other contexts. Using this language can help you to sound natural. What's more, many of these structures and phrases are useful discourse markers, signalling, for example, organisation of ideas or a critical approach. ▶ 7.5

Explorative Task (ii)

Underline the words and expressions which you wouldn't change in the following text.

Renewable energy has been an area of interest to many since the 1973 OPEC oil embargo. The field, however, has since undergone numerous growth-and-bust cycles. It is currently on the upswing, as evidenced by increased funding in the area, and a renewed sense of urgency to move away from fossil fuels. Solar is one facet of renewable energy, with wind and geothermal being others. The underlying motivation is to take advantage of the Sun's abundant energy by converting it into usable forms, much like photosynthesis in plants. What is needed, though, is an active material or system like chlorophyll that can absorb solar radiation and provide efficient charge separation and/or storage.

(Kuno, 2012: 420)

7.2 Adopting good academic practice: referencing and criticality

Plagiarism is often thought of as 'copying', but a more useful definition is 'uncritical and unacknowledged use of other people's work' (Badge and Scott, 2009).

Explorative Task (i)

*What do you think is meant by 'uncritical' and 'unacknowledged' in this context? Compare your ideas with those in the **Study Box** below.*

Study Box: Critical use of sources

Sometimes, you may need to incorporate a relatively straightforward paraphrase of scientific fact (such as the one in **7.1**) into your own analysis or investigation. However, you will often be required to engage **critically** with your sources. You will need to demonstrate your **analysis** and **interpretation** of those sources, and to accurately convey the exact **sense** or **argument** (the *reasoning* behind the claims, ideas and opinions) contained within them. Also, much academic scientific writing is an act of persuasion, so you will need to show that you have **assessed** and **evaluated** the **validity** of the assertions, claims, and opinions that you encounter, and examined the **credibility** of the explanations, evidence and examples put forward in support of them.

Referencing

You will also need to **acknowledge** the role of others' work in your own writing, which always requires careful referencing, and sometimes requires comment. When you use your sources critically, you will see referencing as a positive thing, allowing you to demonstrate that you have read widely, and can position your own work in a wider academic context. References should add depth, interest and credibility to your work.

Explorative Task (ii)

1) *In the **introduction to a research article** below, the references have been removed. Where do you think the authors might make reference to other sources?*

Insufficient sleep, defined as inadequate or mistimed sleep, is increasingly recognised as contributing to a wide range of health problems. Multiple epidemiological studies have shown that self-reported short sleep duration (defined in most studies as ≤6 h) is associated with negative health outcomes, such as all-cause mortality, obesity, diabetes, cardio-vascular disease, and impaired vigilance and cognition. Laboratory studies, in which the sleep of healthy volunteers was restricted, typically to 4 h for 2–6 d, have identified physiological and endocrine variables that may mediate some of these effects, but in general the mechanisms by which insufficient sleep leads to negative health outcomes remain unidentified.

2) *Now compare your predictions with the complete text below and answer the questions which follow it.*

Insufficient sleep, defined as inadequate or mistimed sleep, is increasingly recognised as contributing to a wide range of health problems (1). Multiple epidemiological studies have shown that self-reported short sleep duration (defined in most studies as ≤6 h) is associated with negative health outcomes, such as all-cause mortality (2), obesity (3), diabetes (4), cardio-vascular disease (5), and impaired vigilance and cognition (6). Laboratory studies, in which the sleep of healthy volunteers was restricted, typically to 4 h for 2–6 d, have identified physiological and endocrine variables that may mediate some of these effects (7), but in general the mechanisms by which insufficient sleep leads to negative health outcomes remain unidentified.

(Moller-Levet *et al.*, 2013)

a) How do the writers indicate that they have analysed, interpreted and evaluated the literature? (Look at the verbs they use – what do they tell us?)
b) How do the writers indicate that they have surveyed the literature on this topic in depth?
c) What part of their analysis of the topic is *not* referenced?
d) Does there appear to be good reason to accept their conclusion?

Explorative Task (iii)

*Look at the **conclusion to a research article** and answer the questions which follow it.*

This study shows that neither recipes created by popular television chefs nor ready meals produced by three leading UK supermarket chains meet national or international nutritional standards for a balanced diet. The recipes seemed to be less healthy than the ready meals on several metrics. Maximum nutritional benefit is likely to be derived from home cooking of nutritionally balanced recipes primarily using raw ingredients, rather than relying on ready meals or recipes by television chefs. Further reformulation of ready meals in line with international nutritional guidelines, and collaboration with television chefs to improve the nutritional quality of their recipes, may also help consumers to achieve a balanced diet.

(Howard *et al.*, 2012)

1) If you were paraphrasing these ideas in the text, which verb would you choose to give an accurate interpretation of the **sense** of the original?

a) Howard *et al.* **imply that/demonstrate that** the recipes created by popular TV chefs are poorer in nutritional value than supermarket ready meals.
b) Howard *et al.* **prove that/conclude that** home cooking using raw ingredients is likely to be the best way to achieve a balanced diet.

    c)   Howard *et al.* **note that/indicate that** supermarket meals are actually healthier than the chefs' recipes in some respects.

    d)   Howard *et al.* **advocate/point to** collaboration with TV chefs and supermarkets to improve the nutritional quality of their products.

2)   Complete the summary below so that it reflects the overall **argument** of the original.

    Howard *et al.* (2012) a)_____ that TV chef recipes were as poor in nutritional value as b)_____. Whilst c)_____ that the promotion of home cooking with raw ingredients is probably the best way to improve people's diet, they suggest that collaboration with TV chefs and d)_____ to improve the nutritional quality of their products could also have a e)_____ impact.

Note that it is not always necessary to mention the author of a research report in the sentence, e.g.

> It has been reported that the nutritional value of the recipes popularised by TV chefs is at least as poor as that of supermarket ready meals (Howard *et al.*, 2012). People looking to improve their diet should not assume that the food prepared by TV chefs is healthy and nutritious (see Howard *et al.*, 2012).

The important thing is to fit the evidence from the source into your own analysis and argument.

This information-focussed referencing is particularly common at the start of a research report, when making very general reference to the literature in order to establish a context, e.g.

> The chemistry of metal diynyl and polyynyl complexes is the focus of current intense activity, with potential applications including the construction of one-dimensional molecular wires and metal containing polymers.[1,2]
>
>   (Brown *et al.*, 2010: 2253)

> Buildings in the city of Adapazari, Turkey, suffered heavy damage during the 1999 earthquake. Much of the devastation was attributed to the failure of the low plasticity non-plastic silts (Donahue et al. 2007) that had been deposited by the Sakarya River in its almost annual flooding of the plain over the past 7,000 years (Bol et al. 2010).
>
>   (Arel and Onalp, 2012: 709)

Explorative Task (iv)

Read the text below and compare the paraphrases which follow. Which paraphrase conveys the sense of the writer's original argument? How does it do this?

> The most obvious differences between different animals are differences of size, but for some reason the zoologists have paid singularly little attention to them. In a large textbook of zoology before me I find no indication that the eagle is larger than the sparrow, or the hippopotamus bigger than the hare, though some grudging

admissions are made in the case of the mouse and the whale. But yet it is easy to show that a hare could not be as large as a hippopotamus, or a whale as small as a herring. For every type of animal there is a most convenient size, and a large change in size inevitably carries with it a change of form.

(Haldane, 1928, in Dawkins, 2008: 54)

Paraphrase A

Zoologists at that time paid little attention to differences of size. This can be seen from zoology textbooks, which give no indication that the eagle is bigger than the sparrow, or the hippopotamus larger than the hare, though they do mention the mouse and the whale. Yet it is easy to show that a hare could not be as big as a hippopotamus, or a whale as small as a herring. There is a most convenient size for every kind of animal and a large change in size carries with it a change of form.

Paraphrase B

In 1928, Haldane noted the lack of attention paid to differences of size in different animals, pointing to the very limited discussion of this issue in the zoology textbooks of the time. He argued that it could be easily demonstrated that each species has 'a most convenient size', and that large differences in size impact on form.

In B, the historical context of Haldane's views is more clearly signalled, and the use of the reporting verbs *noted*, *pointing to* and *argued* more clearly attributes the ideas to the original source. In A, there is no clear indication that the ideas come from someone other than the person paraphrasing.

7.3 Strategies for paraphrase and summary

If you attempt to paraphrase or summarise with the text in front of you all the time, it can lead to the problematic 'word changing' approach discussed in **7.1.2**. Instead, use some of the methods outlined in the study box.

Study Box: Strategies for paraphrase and summary

1) *Note-taking*

    Take notes, but make sure you are expressing them and arranging them in a way that reflects your own thought processes.

    Use the notes to flesh out your own outline/argument, rather than just listing the thoughts of others. ▶ **2.1.1** on planning

---

continued . . .

cont.

2) *'Free writing'*

Read a whole section on an idea, theory, method etc., then sit at your computer and attempt to summarise the main points 'freestyle', i.e. quickly, without stopping or consulting the literature.

This will allow you to work through your own understanding of what you have read.

When you have finished, you can go back to the original to check both your general understanding, and particular facts and figures.

3) *Synthesis* (▶ **7.4**)

Create a diagram or table with headings representing the main points you expect to be covered in the literature, and add the different facts, comments, points of view or evidence from each source as you read (with references), in your own words as far as possible.

Use the diagram/table to synthesise what you have read (i.e. note which sources contain the same information, ideas or opinions, or in which respects the sources differ). This provides a general, rounded view of the literature with the focus on different points and issues rather than on individual studies or writers (though the latter may also sometimes be appropriate).

This approach can help you to organise your work in an interesting way.

Practice (i): Paraphrasing scientific facts

1) *Read the text and complete the student's notes which follow.*

Nanotechnology is the understanding and control of matter at dimensions of roughly 1 to 100 nanometers, where unique phenomena enable novel applications. Encompassing nanoscale science, engineering and technology, nanotechnology involves imaging, measuring, modelling, and manipulating matter at this length scale.

At the nanoscale, the physical, chemical, and biological properties of materials differ in fundamental and valuable ways from the properties of individual atoms or molecules, or bulk matter. Nanotechnology R&D (research and development) is directed toward understanding and creating improved materials, devices, and systems that exploit these new properties.

One area of nanotechnology R&D is medicine. Medical researchers work at micro- and nanoscales to develop new drug delivery methods, therapeutics and pharmaceuticals. To provide some perspective, the diameter of DNA, our genetic material, is in the 2.5 nanometer range, while red blood cells are approximately 2.5 micrometers.

A nanometer is one billionth of a meter; a sheet of paper is about 100,000 nanometers thick.

(Adapted from Nanotechnology Initiative, *What is nanotechnology?*)

Nanotechnology – notes (Nanotechnology Initiative, *What is nanotechnology?* http://www.nano.gov/html/facts/whatIsNano.html)

Definition of nanotechnology:

- 'understanding and 1)_____' of materials at the nanoscale, i.e. at approximately 2)_____ nanometres
- 1 nanometre = one billionth of a 3)_____
- sheer scale understood if we consider the dimensions of a sheet of paper – approximately 100,000 nanometres in 4) _____

Properties of nanomaterials:

- scale determines 5)_____ of materials – at the nanoscale, physical, 6)_____ and biological properties of materials differ from those of atoms, molecules and materials in 7)_____

Applications of nanomaterials:

- goal of nanotechnology – exploit these properties and enable 8)_____ applications
- e.g. medicine; new developments at the nanoscale, at the level of 9)_____, diameter of which = approximately 2.5 nanometres – e.g. medicine – researchers working at micro- and nano-scales to develop new drug delivery methods, therapeutics and pharmaceuticals.

2) *Now use the notes to write a concise paraphrase.*

▶ Model Text 7, Appendix 4

Practice (ii): Reporting Research

1) *Paraphrase the text below using some of the reporting verbs and expressions given:*

acknowledge; draw attention to the fact that; according to; conclude that; note

Actual global emissions of carbon dioxide (CO_2) reached a new record of 34.5 billion tonnes in 2012. Yet, the increase in global CO_2 emissions for that year slowed down to 1.1%, which was less than half the average annual increase of 2.9% over the last decade. This development signals a shift towards less fossil-fuel-intensive activities, more use of renewable energy and increased energy saving.
    (PBL Netherlands Environmental Agency, *Trends in global CO_2 emissions*, 2013)

▶ Model Text 8, Appendix 4

2) *Paraphrase the information without direct reference to the authors.*

▶ Model Text 8, Appendix 4

Practice (iii): Conveying argument

Paraphrase the text below using some of the reporting verbs and expressions given:

argue that; emphasise; explain; according to; attach great importance to; make the connection between; underline the significance of

The principle instrument of the transition from alchemy to chemistry was the balance. The ability to weigh things precisely put into humanity's hands the potential to attach numbers to matter. The significance of the achievement should not go by unremarked, for it is in fact quite extraordinary that meaningful numbers can be attached to air, water, gold, and every other kind of matter. Thus, through the attachment of numbers, the study of matter and the transformations that it can undergo (the current scope of chemistry) was brought into the domain of the physical sciences, where qualitative concepts can be rendered quantitatively and tested rigorously against the theories that surround and illuminate them.

(Atkins, 2013: 2)

▶ Model Text 9, Appendix 4

7.4 Synthesising information from multiple sources

Usually, you will want to gather information from a range of sources instead of just one, and synthesise the information and ideas in those sources. This will show that you have read widely and investigated the facts along with different approaches and viewpoints.

Practice

You are going to write an introduction to the following essay:

Are antibiotics a thing of the past?

1) *Start by noting down what you already know in the table.*

What is an antibiotic?	
How does it work?	
How have antibiotics benefitted society?	
What are the current problems associated with antibiotic use?	

2) *Now use the table to make notes from the texts below.*

- *Select information which is relevant and interesting.*
- *Use your own words, except for technical terms or anything that you think is 'quotable'.*
- *Distinguish between fact and opinion.*
- *Indicate any differences of opinion or perspective.*
- *Add references; indicate where information comes from more than one source.*

Text A

Antibiotics, also known as antibacterials, are types of medications that destroy or slow down the growth of bacteria. The Greek word *anti* means 'against', and the Greek word *bios* means 'life'.

Antibiotics are used to treat infections caused by bacteria. Bacteria are microscopic organisms, some of which may cause illness. The word bacteria is the plural of bacterium.

Such illnesses as syphilis, tuberculosis, salmonella, and some forms of meningitis are caused by bacteria. Some bacteria is harmless, while others are good for us.

(Nordqvist, 2013)

Text B

Antibiotics are drugs used for treating infections caused by bacteria. Also known as microbial drugs, antibiotics have saved countless lives.
Misuse and overuse of these drugs, however, have contributed to a phenomenon known as antibiotic resistance. This resistance develops when potentially harmful bacteria change in a way that reduces or eliminates the effectiveness of antibiotics.

(U.S. Food and Drug Administration)

Text C

It is tempting to think that infections are no longer a widespread cause of death and morbidity. In some places and for some groups, this belief is reasonably valid but elsewhere, despite many advances in infection control and treatment, infectious diseases remain a major threat. New antibiotics are being developed for some conditions, but new and some resurgent viral conditions (such as avian and swine flu, SARS, viral encephalitis, and several others) are of course not amenable to antibiotics, and antivirals are rarely very effective. Moreover, certain 'superbugs', such as MRSAs, are emerging in both hospitals and the community, raising the real threat that antibiotic resistance will become ever more common.

(McCracken and Phillips, 2012: 152)

Text D

The discovery of penicillin in 1929 and streptomycin in 1943 heralded the age of antibiotics, and, coincidentally, the founding of the American pharmaceutical industry. Within a decade after World War II, a number of important antibiotics were discovered and developed for therapeutic use. They became the foundation for the treatment of infectious disease. This, along with the introduction of better hygiene, led to a dramatic reduction in worldwide morbidity and mortality due to bacterial infections.

The period from 1950 to 1960 was truly the golden age of antibiotic discovery, as one half of the drugs commonly used today were discovered in that period. Unfortunately, the increasing use of antibiotics for human and non-therapeutic animal use (growth promotion) led all too soon to the development of resistant bacterial pathogens. Recognizing the correlation between antibiotic use and resistance development, much of subsequent antibiotic research has been devoted to the discovery and design of new compounds effective against the successive generations of resistant pathogens.

(Davies, 2006: 287)

Text E

Britain's most senior medical advisor has warned that the rise in drug-resistant diseases could trigger a national emergency comparable to a catastrophic terrorist attack, pandemic flu or major coastal flooding.

Dame Sally Davies, the chief medical officer, said the threat from infections that are resistant to frontline antibiotics was so serious that the issue should be added to the government's national risk register of civil emergencies.

She described what she called an 'apocalyptic scenario' where people going for simple operations in 20 years' time die of routine infections 'because we have run out of antibiotics'.

(Sample, 2013)

3) *Now use your notes to write your introduction, with references.*

▶ Model Text 10, Appendix 4

7.5 Using your reading to build a bank of common structures and phrases

As mentioned earlier in this chapter, using the exact same (non-technical) structures and phrases as the particular source you are using constitutes plagiarism. However, as you read the literature of your subject, you should try to become aware of common structures and phrases that you could use in the rest of your writing to help you express yourself in a natural way. These may also help you to organise your work and develop a critical voice.

Explorative Task

Look back at the texts on antibiotics and pick out any structures and phrases that could be easily used in other contexts.

Practice

Look at how some of these structures and phrases can be adapted to other contexts; then add an example from your own area of study.

1) **the correlation between** antibiotic use **and** resistance development
   • **the correlation between** drug use **and** hepatitis

_____

2) **Despite many advances in** infection control and treatment, infectious diseases **remain a major threat.**
   • **Despite many advances in** computer science, viruses **remain a major threat.**

_____

3)   This, along with the introduction of better hygiene, **led to a dramatic reduction in** worldwide morbidity and mortality due to bacterial infections.
     - Advances in materials design **led to a dramatic reduction in** fatal car accidents.

4)   **Much of subsequent** antibiotic **research has been devoted to** the discovery and design of new compounds effective against the successive generations of resistant pathogens.
     - **Much of subsequent** cancer **research has been devoted to** the development of vaccines.

5)   **The rise in** drug-resistant diseases **could trigger** a national emergency comparable to a catastrophic terrorist attack, pandemic flu or major coastal flooding.
     - **The rise in** obesity **could trigger** a healthcare crisis.

6)   Misuse and overuse of these drugs, however, have **contributed to a phenomenon known as** antibiotic resistance.
     - The adoption of cloud computing has **contributed to a phenomenon known as** 'information sprawl', in which large volumes of data are hosted outside traditional data centres.

See Academic Phrasebank http://www.phrasebank.manchester.ac.uk/, a useful collection of common structures and phrases taken from a wide range of academic texts.

Textual development: structure, coherence, argument and critical thinking

---

Structure, coherence, argument and critical thinking are all inter-related and key to writing long texts successfully.

- In developing a piece of scientific writing, whether it be an essay, a report, a research review or a research paper, you are required to develop an **argument** supported by **critical thinking** and **logical reasoning**.
- If your argument is to be easily understood, then it must be **clearly structured** and **coherent**.

Every argument, like every text, is unique. However, looking at examples of how other writers have thought their ideas through and put down thoughts on the page can help you to develop the awareness and skills to form clearly structured, coherent, well-reasoned arguments which display your ability to think critically, i.e. to assess and question the facts and ideas you encounter in your research, and to reason logically.

8.1 Structure and coherence

It is important that a long piece of writing has a clear structure, usually indicated through **headings** and **sub-headings**. These should serve to guide the reader **visually** and **conceptually** through the text in a logical, coherent manner.

A long text such as an **essay** or **research review** will have the following basic structure:

Section	Possible contents
Title/Question	
Introduction	an opening statement which gains the reader's interest background information/context (with reference to the literature) question to be addressed and its relevance definitions of key terms outline of the purpose and focus of the essay, and the essay structure, i.e. how you will answer the question
Main body	response to the question divided into sections and/or paragraphs, the content and organisation of which reflect the development of your analysis and reasoning
Conclusion	reference back to initial question concise restatement of your argument and the conclusion you have reached through careful reasoning a note of any limitations to your work a suggestion for further work in the area
References	a detailed list of all the sources you have referred to ▶ **9.1**

You will be required to produce long texts which have a more specified structure, such as a **research report**, for which you are required to perform your own scientific investigations. This will have the following structure:

Section/Heading	Possible contents
Title page	title, subtitle, name, other required details
Contents page	the basic structure of the paper with page numbers for each section
Abstract	a concise summary of the research and results, together with their significance

Section/Heading	Possible contents
Introduction	background information/context definition of key terms analysis of the current literature with specific reference to the **gap** in the current knowledge or the **problem** that your research addresses articulation of the exact **research question** to be investigated (i.e. the question you seek to answer through a particular method of inquiry), its relevance, and the rationale behind it outline of the report structure
Methods/Materials and methods	a detailed account of the procedure you followed in order to obtain your results, given in such a way that it could be replicated by others
Results	a detailed scientific analysis of the outcomes of your research/experiment
Discussion	a discussion of the reasons for your results, together with their meaning and significance
Conclusion (might be included in the discussion section)	reference back to initial research question concise restatement of your findings and your argument, and of the conclusion you have reached through careful reasoning a note of any limitations to your study a suggestion for further research work in the area
References	a detailed list of all the sources you have referred to ▶ 9.1
Appendices	data related to the investigation

Many of the research papers you read in scientific journals will follow a similar basic structure of:

- **Title**
- **Abstract**
- **Introduction**
- **Methods**
- **Results**
- **Discussion**

However, you will find acceptable variation across journals. Make a mental note of the structure of the journal articles you read.

Explorative Task

You are going to read some extracts from a research paper in a journal of chemical engineering.

1) *Before you read, match these words from the text with their definitions (using a dictionary where necessary):*

A

i) application	a) soak something with a substance
ii) raw material	b) the total area of an object's surface
iii) surface area	c) a basic material from which other things are made
iv) impregnate	d) the practical use of a material, technology, etc.
v) grind	e) something that is produced when you are making something else
vi) by-product	f) existing in large amounts
vii) abundant	g) make a substance into a powder using a hard surface

B

i) pore	a) a substance used to increase the rate of a chemical reaction
ii) activated carbon	b) one of many small openings on a solid substance
iii) leach	c) extract soluble components from a solid using a solvent (a liquid that dissolves a substance)
iv) catalyst	d) carbon that has been processed so that it is full of small pores that increase the surface area available for adsorption or chemical reactions
v) residue	e) the protective layer surrounding a cereal seed
vi) bran	f) something that remains after a substance has been removed

2) *Use the language or parts in* **bold** *to match the following extracts from the research paper entitled*

Characteristics of Activated Carbons Derived from Deoiled Rice Bran Residues
(Niticharoenwong *et al.*, 2013)

to the following sections (it isn't necessary to understand all the very technical terms):

Abstract; Introduction; Materials and Methods; Results and Discussion; Conclusion

a) **First**, deoiled rice **was treated with** concentrated sulphuric acid (weight ratio of 1:1), at 150°C for 24 h. **After cooling**, the material **was ground**. The excess acid present on the material **was leached out by washing with** sodium bicarbonate solution (1% w/v) until neutral. **The resulting material was then washed with** distilled water. **After drying at 110°C for 24 h, the treated material was impregnated with** H_2PO_4 or $ZnCl_2$.at 1:1 (w/w), and **then dried at 110°C for another 24 h.**

b) **The research focuses on investigation of the characteristics of** activated carbons derived from deoiled bran residues, a major by-product of the rice bran oil industry. **The preparation of** activated carbon **consists of two steps; the first step is** the pre-carbonised acid leaching (H_2SO_4) process and **the second step is** chemical activation **using** H_2PO_4 or $ZnCl_2$ as an activating agent **for the development of** micropores. **The effects of** preparation parameters **including** the types of activating agent (H_2PO_4 and $ZnCl_2$) **and** temperature of activation **were studied.**

c) Activated carbon **is a well-known material with various applications** on an industrial scale. **For example, it is used for** the purification of gases (Guo and Lua, 2002), the removal of organic pollutants from water (Zhou et al., 2009), the removal of heavy metal from wastewater (Daifullah et al., 2003; Montanher et al., 2005; Singh et al., 2005), and as a catalyst or catalyst support (Bedia et al., 2010; Gu et al., 2010). **Activated carbons that are currently commercially available are expensive, however. Therefore, the search for alternative low-cost bio-based materials, as well as the appropriate processes for the preparation of activated carbons from these abundant resources, has become necessary** (Guo and Lua, 2002; Maite et al., 2007).

d) **Table III shows** the BET surface areas of activated carbons **prepared from** H_2PO_4 and $ZnCl_2$ activation **observed at** different activation temperatures. For H_2PO_4 activation, the BET surface area **slightly increases when** the activation temperature increases from 400° to 700°C. **This was possibly because of** a violent gasification reaction **that may cause** a part of the micropore structure to be destroyed by pores collapsing or combining (Oh and Park, 2002)

e) **This study reports** the preparation of activated carbon from deoiled rice bran residues using H_2PO_4 and $ZnCl_2$ as chemical activating agents. $ZnCl_2$ activation **produces** an activated carbon **with higher** surface area **than** H_2PO_4 **produces.** The maximum surface area of 1404 m^2/g was obtained for $ZnCl_2$ activation at the activation temperature of 400° C, **while** the maximum surface area of the material activated with H_2PO_4 was 1187 m^2/g obtained at the activation temperature of 500°C. **Both** H_2PO_4- and $ZnCl_2$-activated carbons **were found to exhibit** a combination of mostly microporous and partly mesoporous structures. **The results from this study demonstrated that deoiled rice bran residues can be a promising abundant, low-cost material for the preparation of activated carbons. These activated carbons can be used as catalyst supports due to their remarkably high surface areas.**

3) *Which extracts use a) the present tense b) the past tense?*

4) *What do you notice about the verbs in the Methods section?*

5) *Underline the expressions in the Methods section which indicate **sequence.***

6) *Which expressions in the Results and Discussion section:*

   ***refer directly** to results/data*

   ***discuss** results*

7) *Which phrase in the Conclusion introduces **a summary of results?***

8) *Underline words in the Conclusion which indicate **similarities and differences** in the results for the two methods?*

9) *What is the function of the last two sentences in the Introduction and Conclusion?*

10) *Highlight all the **precise measurements** provided.*

▶ **9.5** for more information on presenting measurements in science

> Note how **consistent tense use,** the **clear sequencing of information and analysis,** and the use of the **common organisational structures and phrases associated with each section in a research report** make the texts easy to follow despite the complexity of the science.
>
> See Academic Phrasebank http://www.phrasebank.manchester.ac.uk/ for more structures and phrases commonly used in Introduction, Methods, Results, Discussion and Conclusion sections.

There are other text types which you may be required to produce, such as **lab reports** or **research proposals**. The nature and structure of these will differ in some respects according to the subject and the institution, so always follow the particular guidelines you are given.

8.1.1 Focus on Introductions and Conclusions

Whatever the structure of your text, it should be clearly set out at the beginning and signposted throughout. In longer texts such as dissertations, the **Introduction** should tie in with the **Contents page,** and the **Conclusion** should refer back to the Introduction.

The three things should frame your essay and help give it coherence.

Explorative Task

You are going to look at the beginning of a technical report written by a student at the University of Manchester.

1) *Read the introduction to the report and use it to help you complete the list of contents which precedes it using the following headings and sub-headings:*

The Effects of Surface Treatments and Coatings

The Mechanism of Fatigue

Final Fracture

Surface Roughness

Fatigue Crack Propagation

A Comparison of the Effect of Different Types of Coating on the Fatigue Life of Carbon Steel

Contents

1. Introduction

Fatigue, the tendency of a material, such as metal, to break after being subjected to cyclic loading, has been the subject of research for more than 150 years. It was Wohler who first discovered that metallic parts could continue to work for a long time if they were subjected to a *constant* load below their yield point, but that parts could fail if they were subjected to a *cyclic* load, even if it was below the yield point of the material [1]. Over the course of the 20th century, many fatigue failures were recorded. However, fatigue was considered to be a puzzling phenomenon because the damage could not be seen, and the only indicator of the problem was a hidden crack. A complete solution to the problem of fatigue has not yet been discovered [1].

The process of fatigue failure can be divided into three stages: crack initiation, crack propagation, and then rapid fracture, which leads to failure [2]. The fatigue crack is more likely to initiate at the surface of the material because of surface roughness or marks left during the manufacturing process. These act as stress concentration points. Therefore, surface treatment, such as surface polishing, is very important to prevent or delay fatigue failure [3]. In addition, metals exposed to corrosive environments may also be treated with coatings, which may affect fatigue behaviour.

The objective of this project is to examine the process of fatigue failure in carbon steel, with a view to assessing the role of coatings in combatting this problem. It will begin by outlining the mechanism of fatigue. It will then discuss the source of fatigue, and ways of preventing it, with particular focus on the use of coatings.

2) Highlight the parts of the text which contain:

- *an opening statement*
- *background/context*
- *definitions of key terms*
- *the rationale behind the investigation*
- *the purpose of the project*
- *an outline of the project structure*

3) Does the Introduction prepare the reader for what is to come?

4) How might the Conclusion to this project begin?

The **Conclusion** should refer back directly to the Introduction, e.g.

- The objective of this project was to examine the process of fatigue failure in carbon steel, and to assess the effects of coatings on fatigue behaviour.

Notice the use of the past tense.

It should then summarise the findings and the argument, e.g.

- The evidence shows/suggests that ...
- It was found that ...
- It can be concluded that ...

It should then mention the significance or implications of the findings, e.g.

- The findings are significant in that they ...
- The implications of these findings are that ...

It may then indicate any limitations to the current study and suggest areas worthy of further research, e.g.

- The scope of this study was limited to ...
- This study focused on ...
- x would benefit from further study.
- Further study on x may reveal/establish/confirm ...

8.1.2 Describing methodology

Practice

1) *Complete the text from the Methodology section of a paper with the correct form of the verbs below, taking care to consider which of them need to be passive:*

   focus; spend; have; release; feed; observe

   The observations via infrared thermography a) _____ on the elephant group at the Vienna Zoo, Austria. T_s (skin temperature) of four adult female elephants and two juvenile elephants b) _____. The keepers c) _____ direct contact with the group for approximately 1.5 h per day. The elephants d) _____ the night unchained in the indoor enclosure within the family and e) _____ to their outdoor enclosure for approximately 4 h during the day. The elephants f) _____ with hay, branches, carrots and apples.

   (Weissenbock *et al.*, 2010: 182)

2) *Complete the sentences with the correct preposition.*
    a) The solution was heated _____ 150°C.
    b) The environment was kept _____ a steady temperature _____18°C.
    c) The glass was treated _____ corrosive acids to produce a matt finish.
    d) The elephants were enclosed _____ 1pm and 4pm.
    e) The patients attended physical therapy from 11am _____ 1pm each day.

3) *Put the words in order to make sentences describing methodology.*
    a) material/the/cut/was/into/strips/2 cm

    _____

    b) the/cooling/was/mixed/after/solution/with/10 ml/water/of

    _____

    c) months/the/installed/system/was/alarm/throughout/the/and/building/then/monitored six/for

    _____

    d) corrosion/to/prevent/metal/the/was/with/a/coating/treated

    _____

    e) conducted/post-natal/were/using/surveys/email/groups/and/focus

    _____

Study Box: Common structures in methods sections

To do X, Y was done.

Y was done to do X.

X was done (by) using Y.

After/Before _____ ing, X was done.

Prior to X, Y was done.

8.1.3 Describing and discussing results

Practice

1) *Complete these sentences from the results and discussions sections of a paper entitled*

Nutritional quality of organic foods: a systematic review

(Dangour *et al.*, 2009)

with the phrases provided:

> *several strengths; were significantly higher (× 2); beyond the scope of; found no evidence of; it is unlikely that; are comparable; there is no evidence to support*

Results

a) Analysis of satisfactory-quality crop studies _____ a difference in 8 of the 11 nutrient categories.
b) Nitrogen contents _____ in conventionally produced crops, and contents of phosphorus and titratable acidity _____ in organically produced crops.

Discussion

c) The analysis presented suggests that organically and conventionally produced foods _____ in their nutrient content.
d) _____ consumption of these nutrients at the concentrations reported in organic foods in this study provide any health benefit.
e) This review had _____, such as its systematic and exhaustive nature, its broad inclusion criteria, and its methodological rigor.
f) The potential for any benefits to public health [...] warrant further systematic review, but [this] was _____ the current report.
g) One broad conclusion to draw from this review is that _____ the selection of organically produced foodstuffs over conventionally produced foodstuffs to increase the intake of specific nutrients or nutritionally relevant substances.

2) *Which of the above sentences make reference to the following?*

- *specific findings based on data*
- *general findings*
- *the implications of the findings*
- *the strengths of the study*
- *limitations of the study*
- *the need for further research*

▶ 9.3 for common phrases when referring to tables and figures

8.2 Maintaining coherence

Just as the ideas in paragraphs need to be connected, so too do the ideas in a longer text made up of a number of paragraphs and sections. Headings and sub-headings, the **explicit structure** of the text, together with a clear Introduction, can help to guide the reader though the text. However, there must also be an **implicit internal logic**, reflected in the way the points or ideas are organised and connected, which guides the reader through your description, analysis or argument. This involves logical ordering of paragraphs with clear transitions (explicitly signalled, or just clear from the context), and good use of repetition to guide the reader. It is very important to think about how you begin and end paragraphs. It is also important that you signal the importance of the points you wish to foreground or emphasise so that the reader is alerted to them.

Explorative Task

1) *What do you understand by the term 'masonry'?*

2) *Read the text on masonry and complete the table which follows from the list below:*

   history; definition; main techniques; technical analysis on a key point; basic principle

Paragraph 1

Over the last three decades the term 'masonry' has been widened from its traditional meaning of structures built of natural stone to encompass all structures produced by stacking, piling or bonding together discrete chunks of rock, fired clay, concrete, etc., to form the whole. 'Masonry' in **this wider sense** is what these chapters are about. In contemporary construction most masonry in the UK is built from man-made materials such as bricks and blocks. Stone, because of its relatively high cost and the environmental disadvantages of quarrying, is mainly used as a thin veneer cladding or in conservation work on listed buildings and monuments.

Paragraph 2

Second to wood, masonry is probably the oldest building material used by man; it certainly dates from the ancient civilisations of the Middle East and was used widely by the Greeks and Romans. Early cultures used mud building bricks, and very little of their work has survived, but stone structures such as the Egyptian pyramids, Greek temples and many structures made from fired clay bricks have survived for thousands of years. The Romans used both fired clay bricks and hydraulic (lime/ pozzolana) mortar and spread this technology over most of Europe.

Paragraph 3

The basic principle of masonry is of building stable bonded (interlocked) stacks of handleable pieces. The pieces are usually chosen or manufactured to be of a size and weight that one person can place by hand but, where additional power is available, larger pieces may be used, which give potentially more **stable** and durable structures. This greater **stability** and durability is conferred by the larger weight and inertia, which increase the energy required to remove one piece and make it more resistant to natural forces such as winds and water as well as human agency.

Paragraph 4

There are four main techniques for achieving **stable** masonry:

1) Irregularly shaped and sized but generally laminar pieces are selected and placed by hand in an interlocking mass (e.g. dry stone walls).
2) Medium to large blocks are made or cut very precisely to one or a small range of interlocking sizes and assembled to a basic grid pattern either without mortar or with very thin joints (e.g. ashlar or thin-joint).
3) Small to medium units are made to normal precision in a few sizes and assembled to a basic grid pattern, and inaccuracies are taken up by use of a packing material such as mortar (e.g. normal brickwork).
4) Irregularly shaped and sized pieces are both packed apart and bonded together with adherent mortar (e.g. random rubble walls).

Type (4) structures and thin-joint systems depend significantly on the mortar for their stability; all **the other types** rely largely on the mechanical interlocking of the pieces. *Figure V.1* shows typical examples.

Paragraph 5
These descriptions are given to emphasise that most traditional masonry owes much of its strength and stability to interlocking action, weight and inertia while the mortar, when present, is not acting as a glue but as something to fill in the gaps resulting from the imperfect fitting together of the pieces. Most contemporary masonry is type (3) and although modern mortars **do** have an adhesive role much of the strength still derives from mass and friction between interlocking shapes; it is important to remember **this** in design.

(a)

(b)

(c)

(d)

Fig V.1 *The main types of masonry: (a) dry stone wall, (b) ashlar stonework, (c) jointed brick and block work, (d) rubble masonry*

(Domone and Illston, 2010: 247–248)

Paragraph	Content
Paragraph 1	
Paragraph 2	
Paragraph 3	
Paragraph 4	
Paragraph 5	

3) *Does the text have a logical structure?*
4) *Did you find it easy to move from one paragraph to the next?*
5) *Which word is repeated in the first sentence of all the paragraphs? Why do you think this is?*
6) *How do the expressions in bold help to link different parts of the text?*
7) *Which words/phrases does the writer use to give focus to his analysis in the last paragraph?*
8) *Does the inclusion of the photographs enhance your understanding of the text?*

It is clear that sentences at the beginning of a paragraph can connect both to what comes next and what has gone before in the previous paragraph.

Practice

1) *What do you understand by the term 'bioweapons'?*
2) *Read the following text and decide which of these sentences fits at the beginning of each paragraph, underlining any words or phrases which help you:*

   a) *Perhaps more importantly, the initial symptoms may not lead health care providers to suspect bioterrorism.*
   b) *Biological attacks have occurred throughout history and are likely to continue in the future.*
   c) *The biggest consequence of a bioterrorist attack may not be the physical casualties but the psychological impact.*

Paragraph 1

_____

Bioweapons are cheaper to produce than chemical weapons and can cause mass destruction. Several countries have established bioweapons programs for experimentation, and a number of other countries are suspected of possessing harmful biological agents. Additionally, individuals who possess knowledge of genetic engineering could alter simple biological agents to make them more virulent and resistant to antibiotics.

Paragraph 2

_____

Just a few casualties, as seen in the 2001 anthrax attacks, could cause alarm. Even suspicion of a biological weapon being released could instigate mass panic and disruption of communities, health care systems, and governments.

Paragraph 3

_____

As a result, proper precautions may not be taken at first, potentially increasing the number of people exposed and infected. A few initial exposures could quickly turn into mass casualties, especially when the infection is one that can be transferred through human contact.

(Adapted from Strelkauskas et al., 2010: 666)

3) *How do the opening sentences of each paragraph focus the reader on the topic in that paragraph or on particular points?*

4) *Which opening sentence refers back to the preceding paragraph?*

5) *Complete the sentences to summarise the different strands of the argument developed in the text.*

   a) Bioweapons constitute a real threat in today's society **as** _____
   b) **One reason** bioweapons are so dangerous **is that** they not only cause physical damage, _____
   c) **Moreover**, the effects of bioweapons can be difficult to deal with **because** _____

8.3 Building an argument

An argument must be supported by **logical reasoning** demonstrating **critical thinking**. Building an argument will involve supporting the statements you make by providing **explanation, evidence** or **examples**. These will come from your own data or from the **sources** you have assessed. The latter are indicated through **references**.

Explorative Task (i)

1) *Read the passage and complete the table which follows.*

Owing to its enormous body mass, the small surface-to-volume ratio and the lack of sweat glands (Spearman, 1970; Hiley, 1975; Wright, 1984; Mariappa, 1986), elephants are confronted with unusual problems concerning heat dissipation and drying of the integument (Lillywhite and Stein, 1987). Control of skin temperature is an extremely important mechanism in elephants' temperature regulation (Phillips and Heath, 1995) and the most important thermoregulatory organs to use this pathway are the elephants' ears. The ears of the African elephant have a large surface-to-volume ratio as well as an extensive and prominent vascular supply, which predestines these organs for optimal heat dissipation (Wright, 1984).

(Weissenbock et al., 2010: 182)

Statement	Support (the reasons for this)	Source
Elephants find it difficult to keep cool.		
The ears of an elephant are the most important organ for regulating its temperature.		

2) *Which words or phrases are used to indicate the reasons given?*
3) *Read the passage below and complete the table which follows.*

> Overweight and obesity are major threats to public health globally. One estimate suggests that 1.46 billion adults worldwide were overweight in 2008,[1] and projections suggest that by 2020 over 70% of adults in the United Kingdom and United States will be overweight.[2] This is likely to result in millions of additional cases of diabetes and heart disease and thousands of additional cases of cancer.[2]

> 1. Finucane MM, Stevens GA, Cowan MJ, Danaei G, Lin JK, Paciorek CJ, et al. National, regional, and global trends in body-mass index since 1980: systematic analysis of health examination surveys and epidemiological studies with 960 country-years and 9·1 million participants. Lancet 2011;377:557–67.
> 2. Wang YC, McPherson K, Marsh T, Gortmaker SL, Brown M. Health and economic burden of the projected obesity trends in the USA and the UK. Lancet 2011;378:815–25.

(Howard *et al.*, 2012)

Statement	Premise (assumed fact behind the claim)	Support (statistical evidence for the premise)	Source
Overweight and obesity are major threats to public health globally.	Large numbers of people are overweight/obese.		

4) *Read the passage below and complete the table which follows.*

> Infectious diseases remain a major threat to global animal and human health. Recent examples include the 2002 Foot and Mouth Disease outbreak in the UK, the 2003 global epidemic of SARS and the threat of an influenza pandemic. The control of infectious diseases in animals and humans is a problem that needs to be addressed by scientists, veterinarians, healthcare workers, economists, social scientists and policy makers.

(Adapted from *The Royal Society*)

Statement	Support (examples)

At the start of a research report in a dissertation or journal article, the writer must build an argument to justify the research they have undertaken. It is important to develop this argument through the text in a coherent manner.

Explorative Task (ii)

You are going to read a longer extract from the Introduction from a research paper you looked at in 8.1.

1) *Look at the title of the paper and list the things you think might be covered in the opening paragraphs.*

Characteristics of Activated Carbons Derived from Deoiled Rice Bran Residues

  i) _____

  ii) _____

  iii) _____

2) *Read the text and check if the things you chose are mentioned.*

Introduction

Activated carbon is **a well-known material with various applications on an industrial scale.** For example, it is used for the purification of gases (Guo and Lua, 2002), the removal of organic pollutants from water (Zhou et al., 2009), the removal of heavy metal from wastewater (Daifullah et al., 2003; Montanher et al., 2005; Singh et al., 2005), and as a catalyst or catalyst support (Bedia et al., 2010; Gu et al., 2010). **Activated carbons that are currently commercially available are expensive, however. Therefore, the search for alternative low-cost bio-based materials, as well as the appropriate processes for the preparation of activated carbons from these abundant resources, has become necessary** (Guo and Lua, 2002; Maite et al., 2007).

In principle, **the methods for preparing the activated carbons can be divided into two categories: physical activation and chemical activation** (Ahmadpour and Do, 1996). **In physical activation**, a raw material is first carbonized and the carbonized material is then activated by steam (Li et al., 2008), carbon dioxide (Guo et al., 2009), air (Su et al., 2006), or their mixture. **In chemical activation**, a raw material is impregnated with an activation agent such as an acid while being heat-treated under inert atmosphere (Basta et al., 2009; Guo et al., 2002; Liou and Wu, 2009). Often **combinations of chemical activation followed by physical activation methods** are employed to improve the characteristics of activated carbon, such as surface area and pore volume (Azevedo et al., 2007). It has been widely accepted that **activated carbons prepared using different types of raw materials, activation processes, types of precursors, or compositions and process conditions result in different textural and functional characteristics.** For example, activated carbons derived from coconut shell with air activation have a surface area of 700 m^2/g (Su et al., 2006), while steam activation gives a maximum surface area of 1,962 m^2/g (Li et al., 2008), CO_2 activation gives a maximum surface area of 1700 m^2/g (Guo et al., 2009), and chemical activation with $ZnCl_2$ followed by physical activation gives a maximum surface area of 2,114 m^2/g (Azevedo et al., 2007).

Thailand is the sixth largest rice producer in the world ...

(Niticharoenwong *et al.*, 2013: 1309–1310)

Refer to the language in bold to answer the following questions:

3) *How does the first paragraph:*

    a) *establish the importance of the topic?*
    b) *draw attention to a current problem?*
    c) *state the need for a solution?*
    d) *prepare the ground for a discussion of the role of rice as a potential solution to the problem?*

4) *Which phrases link the first and second paragraphs?*

5) *In the second paragraph:*

    a) *How many separate points are covered?*
    b) *What are they?*
    c) *Which phrases and punctuation help to organise the points?*

6) *How do you expect the third paragraph to continue? How do the preceding paragraphs prepare for this?*

7) *Complete the sentence below to describe the **argument** that the authors develop in the paper as a whole:*

    The characteristics of activated carbons derived from deoiled rice bran residues make rice a p _____ raw material for the p _____ of activated carbon.

8) *Match the sentence halves below to summarise the **reasoning behind the argument**.*

a) Activated carbon is a useful material,	we need to find ways of lowering the cost of production.
b) **As** it is expensive to produce,	
c) Using low-cost bio-based materials would help reduce the cost of production,	**Therefore**, if it turns out to be suitable for the production of deactivated carbon, there will be a plentiful supply of raw material.
d) Different processes work differently with different materials, affecting the characteristics of the finished product.	**so** rice, as a relatively cheap biological product, might be a good alternative.
	so we need to produce more of it.
e) Rice is abundant in Thailand.	**For this reason**, it will be interesting to see how rice reacts.

9) *How do the authors support their reasoning to produce a credible argument?*

Practice: Critical thinking

1) *What areas/sources could you investigate to find useful support (evidence; examples) for the statement below in **bold**?*

    Actual global emissions of carbon dioxide (CO_2) reached a new record of 34.5 billion tonnes in 2012. Yet, the increase in global CO_2 emissions for that year slowed down to 1.1%, which was less than half the average annual increase of 2.9% over the last decade. **This development signals a shift towards less fossil-fuel-intensive activities, more use of renewable energy and increased energy saving.**

(PBL Netherlands Environmental Agency, *Trends in global CO$_2$ emissions*, 2013)

2) *What arguments could you put forward to **support** or **challenge** the following statements?*

a) People should adopt a vegetarian diet.
b) Social media such as Facebook and Twitter improve our lives.
c) Governments should invest in nuclear power.
d) It should be compulsory for all students to study scientific subjects until the age of 16.
e) It is important for scientists to be good communicators.

3) *What is the reasoning behind your arguments?*
4) *What kind of evidence would support your arguments?*
5) *What examples could you use to support your arguments?*
6) *How would you structure your argument in a coherent manner?*

8.4 Focus on defining terminology

A coherent text is one which guides the reader through a logical argument. As you do this, you will be required to define some scientific and technical terms. This will aid the non-expert reader, or show an expert reader (i.e. the person assessing your work) that you understand the terminology and have considered any problems or controversies associated with it.

Explorative Task

1) *Look again at the opening paragraph from **8.2** and underline any expressions used to define the term 'masonry'.*

Over the last three decades the term 'masonry' has been widened from its traditional meaning of structures built of natural stone to encompass all structures produced by stacking, piling or bonding together discrete chunks of rock, fired clay, concrete, etc., to form the whole.

2) *Look at some more definitions and underline phrases used to give definitions.*

a) Durability can be defined as the ability of a material to remain serviceable for at least the required lifetime of the structure of which it forms a part.
b) The term mammal encompasses a huge variety of animals, including humans.
c) In today's scientific realm, the prefix 'nano' describes physical lengths that are on the order of a billionth of a meter long (i.e. 10^{-9} m).

Study Box: Useful phrases/structures for defining terminology

A dam **is** a wall **that/which is** built across a river to stop the water from flowing, especially in order to form a lake or produce electricity. ▶ **4.2.4 Focus on relative clauses**

Sharks **are a type of** fish **characterised by** a cartilaginous skeleton.

Durability **can be defined as** the ability of a material to remain serviceable for at least the required lifetime of the structure of which it forms a part.

Psychology **may be defined as** the study of the mind.

The term global warming **refers to** a general increase in global temperatures caused by increased amounts of carbon dioxide around the Earth.

The term mammal **encompasses** a huge variety of animals, including humans.

In today's scientific realm, **the** prefix 'nano' **describes** physical lengths **that** are on the order of a billionth of a meter long (i.e. 10^{-9} m).

Over the last three decades **the term** 'masonry' **has been widened from its traditional meaning of** structures built of natural stone **to encompass** all structures produced by stacking, piling or bonding together discrete chunks of rock, fired clay, concrete, etc., to form the whole.

Practice (i)

Write definitions for the terms below, using some of the phrases in the study box, and being careful to 'add grammar' such as articles and verbs forms.

1) vitamin _____

2) mathematics _____

3) solar panel _____

4) computer virus _____

Practice (ii)

Write some definitions for terms in your own subject, including one which has changed or is problematic.

Review Task

*Write a text on one of the arguments you put forward in **8.3**. Consider how to develop your argument coherently, with logical reasoning. Define any terms where you think it would be helpful for the reader.*

Academic and scientific conventions

Adopting common academic and scientific conventions will help the reader to follow your work more easily.

9.1 Referencing conventions

In **Chapter 7**, you looked at the importance of good practice when referring to sources. In this section you will examine the various conventions associated with referencing. It is very important to reference clearly in order to:

- demonstrate your use of the literature in the field
- allow a reader to find the source easily if they wish to investigate further or double check a fact
- avoid plagiarism

Two systems of referencing can be found in university science departments and scientific journals. In the task below, we will look at some examples.

Explorative Task (i)

Look at the journal extracts and answer the questions which follow.

Text A

In terms of heat regulation the largest terrestrial animal – the elephant – is a case in point. Owing to its enormous body mass, the small surface-to-volume ratio and the lack of sweat glands (Spearman, 1970; Hiley, 1975; Wright, 1984; Mariappa, 1986), elephants are confronted with unusual problems concerning heat dissipation and drying of the integument (Lillywhite and Stein, 1987). Control of skin temperature (T_s) is an extremely important mechanism in elephants' temperature regulation (Phillips and Heath, 1995) and the most important thermoregulatory organs to use this pathway are the elephants' ears. The ears of the African elephant (*Loxodonta africana*) have a large surface-to-volume ratio as well as an extensive and prominent vascular supply, which predestines these organs for optimal heat dissipation (Wright, 1984). In conjunction with their great importance in thermoregulation, the ears are frequently termed "thermal windows" (Wright, 1984; Williams, 1990). Thermal windows are body areas responsible for heat exchange. This is achieved by modifying and controlling blood flow (via vasoconstriction and vasodilation) into these areas (Sumbera *et al.*, 2007).

(Weissenbock *et al.*, 2010: 182)

1) How are sources indicated?
2) How are multiple sources listed and punctuated?
3) What does *et al.* mean?

Text B

In subtropical Hong Kong, most of the electricity consumed in commercial buildings is used for creating a thermally and visually comfortable built-environment through air conditioning and artificial lighting. Recent work on computer energy-simulation studies for Hong Kong revealed that air-conditioning accounts for over 50% of the total electricity consumption in commercial buildings and electric lighting comes second with 20–30% [1]. Passive solar design and daylighting, which makes use of natural light to reduce electric lighting energy consumption, have long been recognized as potential energy-efficient design strategies for buildings [2,3].

(Danny *et al.*, 2007: 1199–1200)

1) How are sources indicated?
2) How are multiple sources listed and punctuated?

Text C

The current WHO definition of health, formulated in 1948, describes health as "a state of complete physical, mental and social well-being and not merely the absence of disease or infirmity."[1] At that time this formulation was groundbreaking because of its breadth and ambition. It overcame the negative definition of health as absence of disease and included the physical, mental, and social domains. Although the definition has been criticised over the past 60 years, it has never been adapted. Criticism is now intensifying,[2-5] and as populations age and the pattern of illness changes the definition may even be counterproductive.

(Huber *et al.*, 2011)

1) How are sources indicated?
2) How are multiple sources listed and punctuated?

Referencing systems

1) Text A refers to sources using surnames and dates, e.g.

   (Wright, 1984)

This is known as the **Harvard system**.

The name and date are usually separated by a comma.

If the reference accompanies a quotation (▶ **9.2**), a page number is included, preceded by a colon, or in some cases a comma, e.g.

   (Wright, 1984: 32)

Multiple references usually occur in chronological order separated by semicolons, e.g.

   (Spearman, 1970; Hiley, 1975; Wright, 1984; Mariappa, 1986)

A source with two authors is presented with both names joined with *and*, e.g.

   (Phillips and Heath, 1995)

Sources with more than two authors include the name of the lead author followed by *et al.*, which means 'and others', e.g.

   (Sumbera *et al.*, 2007)

Note that *et al.* is often italicised

   (Sumbera *et al.*, 2007)

2) Texts B and C use a number system to refer to sources; this is known as the **Vancouver system**. In practice, there is variation in the presentation of numbers.

They can occur:

in parentheses, e.g.

   ... electric lighting comes second with 20–30% (1).

in square brackets, e.g.

   ... electric lighting comes second with 20–30% [1].

as superscript numbers, e.g.

   ... electric lighting comes second with 20–30% .[1]

or with superscript numbers in round/square brackets, e.g.

   ... electric lighting comes second with 20–30%.[1]

Note that bracketed numbers come before punctuation marks, while superscript numbers come after any punctuation marks.

Multiple sources are separated by a comma, e.g.

… strategies for buildings [1,2].

A dash is used with a consecutive string of sources, e.g.

Criticism is now intensifying,[2-5] …

Both systems occur in academic scientific writing, although the Vancouver system is more common. The type of referencing system you use will depend on guidelines issued by a particular institution or publication. What is most important is that you follow any guidelines you are given carefully, and that your references are **complete, accurate and consistent**.

The referencing system you use will also determine the way you present your references at the end of your text.

Explorative Task (ii)

1) *Which system is being followed in these lists of references?*

A

Atkins, P. (2013) *What Is Chemistry?* Oxford: Oxford University Press.

Davies, J. (2006) Where have all the antibiotics gone? *Canadian Journal of Infectious Diseases and Medical Microbiology*, 17(5), 287–290.

Dinwoodie, J. (2010) Timber, in P. Domone and J. Illston (eds) *Construction Materials: their Nature and Behaviour*, (4th Edition), Oxon: Spon Press, 403–506.

Housecroft, C. and E. Constable (2010) *Chemistry: An Introduction to Organic, Inorganic and Physical Chemistry*, (4th Edition), Harlow: Pearson Education.

Rincon, P. (2011) *How sticky tape led to the Nobel Prize*, BBC, 5th October, http://www.bbc.co.uk/news/science-environment-11478645 [accessed 4th March, 2013].

Royal Society, http://royalsociety.org [accessed 20th November, 2012].

B

1. J. Davies, Where have all the antibiotics gone? Canadian Journal of Infectious Diseases and Medical Microbiology, 2006, 17(5), 287–290.

2. Royal Society, http://royalsociety.org [accessed 20th November, 2012].

3. J. Dinwoodie, Timber, in P. Domone and J. Illston (eds) Construction Materials: their Nature and Behaviour, (4th Edition), Oxon: Spon Press, 2010, 403–506.

4. P. Atkins, What Is Chemistry? Oxford: Oxford University Press, 2013.

5. C. Housecroft and E. Constable, Chemistry: An Introduction to Organic, Inorganic and Physical Chemistry, (4th Edition), Harlow: Pearson Education, 2010.

6. P. Rincon, How sticky tape led to the Nobel Prize, BBC, 5th October, 2011, http://www.bbc.co.uk/news/science-environment-11478645 [accessed 4th March, 2013].

2) *What are the main differences between the two lists?*

3) *What do you notice about the punctuation?*

4) *What extra information is given for websites?*

 Harvard system

References are listed in alphabetical order, according to the surname of first author, whose surname must come before the first name or initial. (There is no need to reverse the other names as there is no alphabetical consideration, but some do.)

The date follows the name, at the beginning.

Vancouver system

References are listed in numerical order according to where they appear in the text (with the first name or initial followed by the surname – there is no need to reverse as there is no alphabetical consideration, but some do).

The date comes at the end, but before any volume/issue/page numbers.

Note the inclusion of the URL and the date accessed for websites.

Both the reference lists above are presented with typical punctuation and formatting regarding the use of brackets, commas, colons and italics. However, within the parameters of each system there is a certain amount of acceptable variation depending on the subject/institution/publication, for example:

- Some use first names, others use initials.
- Some reverse all names, others only the first name in a Harvard reference.
- Some use italics for the titles of books and journals, others do not.
- Some use quotation marks for article and chapter titles, others do not.
- Some put the date in brackets, others do not.
- Some separate the place of publication and the publisher with a colon, others use a comma.

The most important thing is to follow the guidelines you are given and to make sure your references are **complete, accurate and consistent**.

Note that some subjects have very specific conventions. See for example the absence of title, the use of standard abbreviations for journal titles, and the use of bold for the journal volume in the following references from *Chemistry*, following *Royal Society of Chemistry* guidelines:

1) R. L. Beddoes, C. Bitcon and M. W. Whitely, *J. Organomet. Chem.*, 1991, **402**, 85.
2) O. F. Koentjoro, R. Rousseau and P. J. Low, *Organometalics*, 2001, **20**, 4502.
3) P. J. Low and M. I. Bruce, *Adv. Organomet. Chem.*, 2001, **48**, 71.

5) *Identify the following in the above reference lists and note which details are included:*

    a) a book (with one edition)
    b) a book (with several editions)
    c) a chapter from a book
    d) a journal article
    e) a website document/article
    f) a website

9.2 Incorporating quotation

The use of direct quotation is relatively rare in the sciences in comparison with other academic disciplines. However, it can be useful, particularly when defining terms. If used, it should be carefully incorporated into the grammar of the sentence, e.g.

> Complementary and alternative medicine (CAM) can be defined as 'diagnosis, treatment, and/or prevention which complements mainstream medicine by contributing to a common whole, by satisfying a demand not met by orthodoxy or by diversifying the conceptual frameworks of medicine'.[1]

> McDougal has also observed that the prevailing approach surrounding questions of reproductive decision-making is "based on the notion of the primacy of parental procreative liberty" (2005, 601).

Notice that the punctuation comes outside the quote as it is not a complete sentence, and that the page number is included in the reference (preceded by a colon or comma).

Sometimes, you may not need to use a long string of quotation, just key phrases, e.g.

> Complementary and alternative medicine (CAM) can be defined as 'diagnosis, treatment, and/or prevention' complementing orthodox medicine. It contributes to 'a common whole' by fulfilling a need not met by traditional medicine or by 'diversifying the conceptual frameworks of medicine'.[1]

If the quotation is a full sentence, it should be introduced with a colon, e.g.

> McDougal makes the following observation: "The current approach surrounding questions of reproductive decision-making is based on the notion of the primacy of parental procreative liberty." (2005, 601)

Notice that the punctuation comes within the quote as it is a complete sentence.

A longer 'block quotation' should also be introduced with a colon and indented, and should have no quotation marks. It may also have a different format to the rest of the text: the font size may be smaller and the line spacing reduced, as stipulated in the guidelines of the institution or publisher. The reference follows the quote (after the final full stop), e.g.

> Other potential risks of harm raised in the debate relate to the psychological impact on the child in knowing that he or she was selected on the basis of his or her particular characteristics (in this case, on the basis of tissue type) (see Ram 2006, 280). Stephen Wilkinson summarizes these as follows:
>
>> There seem to be two linked but analytically separate concerns here: first, that a future child may suffer psychological harm if she finds out that she was not wanted for herself, but as a means to save the life of a sibling; and, second, that a child conceived for this reason is likely to enjoy a less close and loving relationship with its parents. (2010, 113)

Note from the examples given that both single and double quotation marks occur in scientific journals. Follow the guidelines given by your department. If there are no guidelines on this, just make sure you are consistent.

Sometimes, not everything in a quote will be relevant or necessary. You can indicate that you have left something out with ellipses, in square brackets (to make it clear that it is you, and not the quoted writer who is omitting something), e.g.

> Complementary and alternative medicine (CAM) can be defined as 'diagnosis, treatment, and/or prevention which complements mainstream medicine [...] satisfying a demand not met by orthodoxy or by diversifying the conceptual frameworks of medicine'.[1]

You can also use square brackets to indicate any changes or additions you have made to the quote to make it fit in with your grammar or sense, e.g.

if the actual quote is:

> It is diagnosis, treatment, and/or prevention which complements mainstream medicine.

you may need to change it to:

> [Complementary and alternative medicine] is diagnosis, treatment, and/or prevention which complements mainstream medicine.

If something is followed by [sic], it means that there is something in the original which is factually or grammatically incorrect.

Practice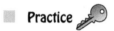

Incorporate the quotations, in full or using some parts, into your own sentences, and reference appropriately.

1) 'Polymers are substances that have macromolecules composed of many repeating units (known as "mers").' (*Oxford Dictionary of Science*, 2005: 648)

   The *Oxford Dictionary of Science* defines _____

2) 'The basic structure of an atom consists of a nucleus surrounded by a cloud of electrons.' (Atkins, 2013: 17)

   The structure of an atom _____

3) 'From Pythagoras to string theory, the desire to comprehend nature has been framed by the Platonic ideal that the world is a reflection of some perfect mathematical form.' (Smolin, 1997, in Dawkins, 2009: 363)

   According to Smolin, _____

4) 'The period from 1950 to 1960 was truly the golden age of antibiotic discovery, as one half of the drugs commonly used today were discovered in this period.' (Davies, 2006: 287)

   Davies describes the period from 1950 to 1960 _____

9.3 Tables and figures

Tables and figures are a useful way of presenting information in an accessible way. When including them, it is important to follow established conventions.

Explorative Task

1) What do you notice about the way these tables and figures are labelled?

Text A: Diagram

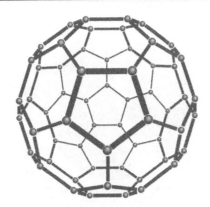

Figure 3.1 Illustration of a C_{60} molecule

C_{60} is a spherical molecule consisting of 60 carbon atoms arranged in a soccer ball shape as shown in **Figure 3.1**.

Figure 9.1

(Kuno, 2012: 30. Reprinted with the kind permission of Garland Science/Taylor and Francis LLC).

Text B: Bar Chart

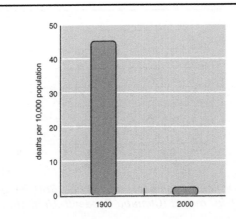

Figure 6.11 An illustration of the changes in deaths caused by infectious diseases over a century in the United States.

Health departments at the local and state levels require that doctors and hospitals report certain diseases. This type of information has been able to show how the effects of infectious diseases have changed over the years (**Figure 6.11**).

Figure 9.2

(Strelkauska et al., 2010: 111. Reprinted with the kind permission of Garland Science/Taylor and Francis LLC)

Text C: Pie Chart

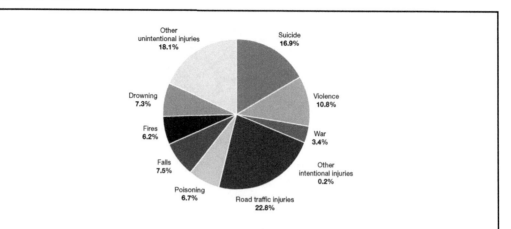

Figure 7.4 Global injury mortality by cause, 2002. Source: WHO, 2004, Fig. 2.1, p.34.

Worldwide, but especially in the developing world, injury and/or accidents are a very important, varied and growing cause of mortality and long-term disability (Figure 7.4).

Figure 9.3

(McCracken and Phillips, 2012: 175. Reprinted with the kind permission of the World Health Organisation)

Text D: Line Graph

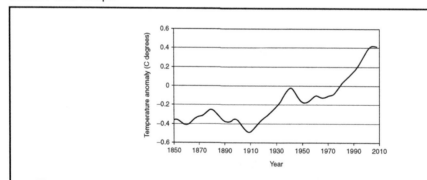

Fig. 62.3 Global surface air temperatures since 1850 Temperature anomaly = difference from 1961-90 mean) (Climatic Research Unit, University of East Anglia, 2009).

Global temperatures are increasing rapidly at a seemingly unprecedented rate (*Fig. 62.3*), but it is worth noting that changes in global temperature and atmospheric carbon dioxide levels are nothing new.

Figure 9.4

(Domone and Illston, 2010: 536. Reprinted with the kind permission of the *Climatic Research Unit*)

Text E: Table

Table 52.4 Average green moisture content of the sapwood and heartwood

Botanical name	Commercial name	Moisture content (%)	
		Heartwood	Sapwood
Hardwoods			
Betula lutea	Yellow birch	64	68
Fagus grandifolia	American beech	58	79
Ulmus americana	American elm	92	84
Softwoods			
Pseudotsuga menziesii	Douglas fir	40	116
Tsuga heterophylla	Western hemlock	93	167
Picea sitchensis	Sitka spruce	50	131

The degree of variation is illustrated for a number of softwoods and hardwoods in *Table 52.4*.

Figure 9.5

(Domone and Illston, 2010: 425)

Text F: Table

Table 9.1 Characteristics of Gram-Positive and Gram-Negative Bacteria

Characteristic	Gram-Positive Bacteria	Gram-Negative Bacteria
Peptidoglycan	Thick layer	Thin layer
Teichoic acid	Present	Absent
Lipids	Very little	Lipopolysaccharide layer
Outer membrane	No	Yes
Toxins	Exotoxins	Endotoxins
Sensitivity to antibiotics	Very sensitive	Moderately sensitive

The difference between the Gram-positive cell wall and the Gram-negative cell wall is significant. **Table 9.1** compares the two types of cell wall.

Figure 9.6

(Strelkauska et al., 2010: 160. Reprinted with the kind permission of Garland Science/ Taylor and Francis LLC)

Tables are labelled at the top; figures are labelled at the bottom.

Note the different types of figure (diagram, bar chart, pie chart, line graph) common in scientific texts. You may also need to make use of other types such as flow charts, and chemical drawings and schemes.

As you can see from the examples, there is some acceptable variation across texts regarding how titles, table headings and figure labels are formatted, though it is common to write **table** and **figure** in bold.

The important thing is to follow any guidelines you have been given and to be clear and consistent.

If the table or figure is taken from another source, it must be referenced using the appropriate system (see Texts C and D).

2) *What expressions in the accompanying texts are used to refer directly to the tables and figures?*

Practice (i)

Use the words below in the right form to complete the following phrases commonly used to

refer to tables and figures:

show; illustrate; list; see; compare; demonstrate

1) The changes in temperature are _____ in **Table 3.8**.
2) **Figure 3** _____ the different shapes of brick available.
3) The results of the experiment can be _____ in **Table 2**.
4) The graph _____ data obtained from four donors.
5) One of the symptoms is a rash, as _____ in **Figure 10.2**.
6) **Table 2** _____ the major differences between the two cell types.

Practice (ii)

1) *Complete the text accompanying the graph with the following verbs in the correct form:*

double; decline

Fig. 62.5 World and UK steel production (World Steel Association, 2009).

World steel production nearly _____ between the mid-1990s and 2008 (*Fig. 62.5*), and is expected to double again by 2050, with some fluctuations due to the global economic conditions (World Steel Association, 2009). Production in the UK _____ by about 40% in the same period.

Figure 9.6

(Domone and Illston, 2010: 541. Reprinted with the kind permission of the *World Steel Association*)

2) *Use the structures from the tables to write more sentences about the graph in 1.*

world/ UK steel production	doubled	steadily	between x and y
	halved	sharply	in the same period
	rose/fell (by)	significantly	
	increased/decreased (by)	slightly	
	went up/down (by)		
	declined		
	plummeted		
	levelled off		
	fluctuated		

there was	a	steady	rise/fall	In world/	between x and y
		sharp	increase/decrease	UK steel	in the same period
		significant	decline	production	
		slight			

1) _____

2) _____

3) _____

4) _____

5) _____

9.4 Equations

Equations are common throughout scientific writing, and it is important to present them clearly.

Explorative Task

1) *What do you notice about the way these equations are introduced, formatted and referenced?*

2) *Which phrases in the accompanying texts are used to refer to the equations directly?*

A

The earth's atmosphere is oxidising. Nearly all of the earth's crust consists of oxides, which indicates that this is the preferred minimum energy state for most materials. Gold and silver are the only two metals that are found in their native, unoxidised state. The general oxidising reaction can be written as:

$$M + O \rightarrow MO \qquad\qquad (10.1)$$

where M is the metal and O is the oxygen.

B

When an element or compound burns in dioxygen to give an oxide, it is *oxidised* (equation 1.42).

$$2Mg(s) + O_2(g) \rightarrow 2MgO(s) \qquad\qquad (1.42)$$

Conversely, if a metal oxide reacts with dihydrogen and is converted to the metal, then the oxide is reduced (equation 1.43).

$$CuO(s) + H_2(g) \xrightarrow{\text{Heat}} Cu(s) + H2O(g) \qquad\qquad (1.43)$$

In reaction 1.42, O_2 is the *oxidising agent* and in reaction 1.43, H_2 is the *reducing agent*.

1) An equation can be integrated into the sentence as in A. In this case, the equation is introduced with a colon, and the sentence continues after the equation (so does not begin with a capital letter).

An equation can also be preceded and followed by complete sentences, as in B.

2) The equation is indented.
3) The equation is referenced on the far right.

Practice

Rewrite the text with the correct formatting and punctuation.

If a soap film is stretched across a frame with a moveable wire, the force required to hold the wire in place is $F = 2yl$ (6.1) where l is the length of the wire, y is the surface tension of the soap film/air interface and the factor 2 is introduced because the film has two surfaces.

▶ Model Text 11, Appendix 4

9.5 Units of measurement

Measurements should be presented following the SI (*Système International d'Unités*). The following are used widely throughout the scientific world. Note the use or non-use of capital letters and spaces in the examples: it is important that you write these correctly.

Measuring length

Unit	Abbreviation	Example
metre	m	100 m
centimetre	cm	50 cm
millimetre	mm	10 mm
nanometre	nm	400 nm

Weighing mass

Unit	Abbreviation	Example
kilogram	kg	40 kg
gram	g	100 g
milligram	mg	20 mg

Measuring volume

Unit	Abbreviation	Example
litre	l	4 l
millilitre	ml	20 ml
cubic metre	m^3	4 m^3

Other generally useful abbreviations

Unit	Abbreviation	Used to measure	Example
degree Celsius	°C	temperature	30°C
square metre	m^2	area	5 m^2
minute	min	time	25 min

Refer to:

International System of Units (2006) Bureau International des Poids et Mesures (8th edition), http://www.bipm.org/utils/common/pdf/si_brochure_8_en.pdf
for other units used in your subject.

Practice

Correct the mistakes in the way the measurements are written.

1) Temperatures may reach 40°c.
2) The wire measured 2mm in diameter.
3) The machine weighs 44 Kg.
4) Measure 2 ls of water.
5) 2 g of solution were added to every m3 of water.

9.6 Acronyms and abbreviations

Acronyms and abbreviations can be useful in academic scientific writing.

- **Acronyms** are formed using the first letter of each word in a phrase, capitalised, e.g.

  The UN (United Nations)
  The RSC (Royal Society of Chemistry)

- **Abbreviations** are formed by shortening a word, e.g.

  esp. (especially)
  etc. (from the Latin *et cetera*, meaning 'and others')

Explorative Task (i)

Look at the text and complete the rule which follows about using acronyms by choosing the correct option.

> The recent uptake of mobile phones has been accompanied by some concern about possible health risks.[1] In the general population, the health effects most often attributed to mobile phone use are non-specific symptoms. Excluding sensations of mild warmth, the most commonly reported symptoms are headache, burning, dizziness, fatigue, and tingling.[2] Mechanisms to explain these phenomena remain speculative, and, although the pulsing nature of 'global system for mobile communication' (GSM) signals has been suggested to be partly to blame,[3] experiments that have exposed healthy adults to GSM signals under blind conditions have not found any significant effects on the reporting of symptoms.[4]
>
> (Rubin, 2006)

> *Rule for acronym use*
>
> When mentioning a term for the first time, use **the full term/the acronym/either** and put **the full term/the acronym/either** in brackets afterwards. After this, always use **the full/ term/the acronym/either**.

Practice

Rewrite the text with correct use of acronyms.

> GM foods are becoming more widely available. Many see the increased production of GM (genetically modified) crops as an important tool in the fight against world hunger. However, others are concerned by the possible effects of these foods on health.

▶ Model Text 12, Appendix 4

Explorative Task (ii)

Identify the abbreviations in these sentences and complete the table below.

1) The report recommends encouraging higher consumption of legumes, e.g. lentils and chickpeas.
2) Atmospheric nitrogen needs to be 'fixed', i.e. converted into a form that can be used by plants.
3) The chapter outlines *common* garden experiments (cf. *contrasting* garden experiments, pp. 45–7).
4) N.B. Protective clothing must be worn at all times.

	Abbreviation	Derivation	Meaning
sentence 1		*exempli gratia*	
sentence 2		*id est*	
sentence 3		*confer*	
sentence 4		*nota bene*	

9.7 Bullet point and numbered lists

Lists with numbers or bullet points are a useful way of organising information. There is some acceptable variation in the formatting of these lists.

Explorative Task

1) *What differences do you notice in the formatting of these lists?*

2) *How are references given?*

A

The desired properties of a sealant are:
- a good adhesion with the joint
- low rate of hardening
- low rate of shrinkage
- permanent elasticity.

B

Much of the output of the construction industry comprises buildings and structures that subsequently consume vast quantities of energy for heating, lighting, maintenance etc. while in service. Over their entire lifespan, structures are responsible for (Toyne, 2007):
- 40% of the world's energy use
- 40% of the world's solid waste generation
- 40% of the world's greenhouse gas emissions
- 33% of resource use
- 12% of water use.

C

Significant health differences between occupational groups are found in all countries. In part these reflect the direct influences on health of workplace hazards. Depending on their particular work environment, workers may be exposed to:
- physical hazards – e.g. heat, noise, radiation, dust, vibration;
- mechanical hazards – e.g. unsafe structures, unshielded machinery;
- chemical hazards – e.g. pesticides, solvents, gases, acids, metals;
- biological hazards – e.g. bacteria, parasites, viruses;
- psycho-social hazards – e.g. stress, monotony, workforce bullying, excessively long working hours; and
- regulatory hazards – e.g. inadequate safety standards, poor enforcement frameworks.

D

There are four main techniques for achieving stable masonry:
1) Irregularly shaped and sized but generally laminar pieces are selected and placed by hand in an interlocking mass (e.g. dry stone walls).
2) Medium to large blocks are made or cut very precisely to one or a small range of interlocking sizes and assembled to a basic grid pattern either without mortar or with very thin joints (e.g. ashlar or thin-joint).

3) Small to medium units are made to normal precision in a few sizes and assembled to a basic grid pattern, and inaccuracies are taken up by use of a packing material such as mortar (e.g. normal brickwork).

4) Irregularly shaped and sized pieces are both packed apart and bonded together with adherent mortar (e.g. random rubble walls).

---

1) The items in the list can be words or phrases which form part of the introductory sentence.

- These are introduced with a colon, and do not start with a capital letter (A, B, C).
- In this case, each item can be unpunctuated, except for the last one, which ends in a full stop as it is the end of the whole sentence (A, B).
- Alternatively, the items before the last can be separated by semi-colons (C).
- Using *and* to join the last two options is optional.

2) Items can sometimes be written as full sentences, each beginning with a capital letter and ending with a full stop (D).

- These can be preceded by a colon or a full stop.

3) References which apply to the whole list should be included in the introductory sentence (B).

Practice

Rewrite the following as a bullet point list.

Newton – 3 laws of motion – first law: a body continues in its state of rest of uniform motion in a straight line unless acted upon by an external force; second law: the rate of change of momentum of a body is proportional to the applied force and takes place in the direction in which the force acts; third law: for every action there is an equal and opposite reaction.

▶ Model Text 13, Appendix 4

Note that the list can also be contained within the main text, e.g.

The elephants were observed in the following defined situations: (1) indoors, (2) outdoors, and (3) return to indoors.

Note the use of the colon, commas and *and*.

9.8 UK versus US spelling

There are a number of spelling differences between UK and US English.

Explorative Task

Add the title UK or US to these lists.

A _____	B _____
colour, behaviour, labour	color, behavior, labor
centre, metre	center, meter
travelling	traveling
prioritise, stabilise	prioritize, stabilize
offence, defence, practice (noun)/practise (verb)	offense, defense, practice (noun and verb)

Which US spelling is also now commonly used in the UK?

It is probably best to use the spelling system used in your country of study. Certain publications may require UK or US spelling. However, the most important thing is to be consistent, and not mix the two.

9.9 Formatting and presentation

It is important that any written work you submit is **professional**, that it is clearly presented, and has clear and consistent formatting. This will show that you have worked with care and attention to detail. It will also make your work easier to read. Different institutions and publications will often provide you with detailed guidelines with respect to this. These will often contain the following basic instructions:

- Use a clear font such as Times New Roman.
- Use 1.5 or double spacing.
- Make titles and sub-titles clear.
- Make sure new paragraphs are clearly separated by leaving a line space, indenting, or both.
- Include page numbers.

APPENDIX

1

Verb forms and patterns

A1.1 Verb forms

When deciding on the correct verb form, there are three main things you need to consider:

- choice of **tense** (present; past)
- choice of **aspect** (perfect; continuous)
- choice of **voice** (active; passive)

Study Box: Common verb forms in academic scientific writing

1) The present is used to convey scientific facts, e.g.

   DNA **contains** genetic information.

   Much of the rain forest **is being destroyed**.

2) The present simple is also used to refer to current ideas in the literature, e.g.

   Gayle **concludes** that extended use of the vaccine in schools would greatly benefit these communities.

   There **is** general consensus on this in the literature.

3) The present perfect is often used to introduce general observations on the literature up to the present day, particularly in introductions, e.g.

   There **has been** a great deal of research on alternative medicine.

   To date, little research **has focussed** on the long-term effects of mobile phone use.

---

continued . . .

cont.

4) The past simple is used to refer to completed actions or states in the past, often combined with a specific time adverbial, e.g.

The first lunar landing **occurred** in 1969.

This use is sometimes linked to the narration of a series of events, along with the past continuous (to give background information), and the past perfect (to refer to a point in time before the current narrative).

The entire world **was watching** when the first humans **landed** on the moon. There **had**, of course, **been** earlier unmanned lunar missions, but the 1969 landing **was** a new milestone in space exploration.

5) The past simple passive is very commonly used to recount the methodology of scientific investigations, e.g.

The solution **was heated** to boiling point.

The subjects **were monitored** over a period of six months.

6) Note the tense use after *if* in conditional sentences.

If the structure **weakens**, the whole building **will collapse**.

(Present tense + WILL DO refers to future time. Denotes possible events/states.)

If people **knew** the risks, they **would not take** this drug.

(Past tense + WOULD DO refers to present time. Denotes unlikely events/states.)

If the government **had implemented** the safety standards earlier, more lives **would have been saved**.

(Past perfect + WOULD HAVE DONE refers to hypothetical event/state in the past.)

Other expressions are also used with the present tense to denote future: *until; in case; provided that.*

Practice (i)

Find the errors in the verb forms and correct them.

1) Water is boiling at 100 degrees Celsius.
2) Ozone found naturally in the Earth's stratosphere.
3) The World Wide Web has been invented in 1990.
4) Many different kinds of plastic were developed in recent years.
5) The effects of the drug have been showed in recent studies.
6) To date, little research is carried out on this area.

Practice (ii)

Write the verbs in the correct form.

1) The sun _____ (rise) in the east and _____ (set) in the west.
2) Pathogenic bacteria _____ (become) increasingly resistant to antibiotics.
3) In 1929, Edwin Hubble _____ (discover) that the universe (expand) _____
   Hubble acknowledged that his discoveries were in many ways dependent on the work
   that _____ (do) by the many astronomers who came before him.
4) Since the early 1980s, developments in genetic engineering _____ (make) it
   possible to produce genetically modified crops.
5) In the initial study, a salt solution _____ (add) to the samples prior to
   centrifugation.

Practice (iii)

Write the verbs in the correct form.

1) The metal should be heated until it _____ (reach) a liquid state.
2) This type of building will not be safe if there _____ (be) an earthquake.
3) If governments _____ (implement) stricter controls on industry, carbon
   emissions _____ (fall), but this does not seem likely at the moment.
4) If the population _____ (vaccinate), the current measles outbreak _____
   (prevent).

Practice (iv): Describing processes

*Complete the text with the correct form of the verbs below, taking care to consider which
of them need to be passive:*

trap; heat; rely; carry; insulate; pump

Solar heating is a form of domestic or industrial heating that 1) _____ on the
direct use of solar energy. The basic form of the solar heater is a thermal device in
which a fluid 2) _____ by the sun's rays in a collector and 3) _____
or allowed to flow round a circuit that provides some form of heat storage and some
form of auxiliary heat source for use when the sun is not shining. The simplest form
of a solar collector is the flat-plate collector, in which a blackened surface covered by
one or more glass plates acts like a greenhouse and 4) _____ the maximum
amount of solar energy. Tubes attached to the receiving surface 5) _____
air, water, or some other fluid to which the absorbed heat is transferred. The whole
panel 6) _____ at the back and can thus form part of the roof of a building.
(*Oxford Dictionary of Science*, 2005: 761)

A1.2 Verb patterns

Many verbs require specific syntactic patterns when they occur in a sentence. See for example the verbs describing cause and effect in the **Study Box**.

Study Box: Cause and effect: verb patterns

x causes/leads to/results in/gives rise to y
x causes y to do sth
x leads/results in y doing sth
x does y/x is done, which ...
x does y/x is done, causing/leading to/resulting in/giving rise to/triggering ...

Practice

Combine the phrases and verbs below to show cause and effect.

1) water pressure → wheel turns (cause)

_____

2) continued use of fossil fuels → climate change (give rise to)

_____

3) the new safety measures introduced last year → decrease in accidents (lead to)

_____

4) better technology in the future → more efficient energy production (result in)

_____

5) dirty drinking water → sickness → national health crisis (result in/trigger)

_____

Complex noun phrases

Whichever type of sentence you use, it will almost always have at least one subject, and possibly an object, and these almost always comprise noun phrases. A noun phrase can be just one word, or several, as shown in the examples below:

- **Research** has been conducted in this area.

- **Research funded by the government** has been conducted in this area.

- **Original research funded by the government** has been conducted in this area.

Explorative Task (i)

Compare the structures below. How do they differ grammatically? Which is more effective? Why?

1) Brown carried out some important research. The research investigated the causes of breast cancer. It was funded by the British Medical Foundation.
2) Brown's important research into the causes of breast cancer was funded by the British Medical Council.

The first one uses several **subject + verb** structures and is quite repetitive; the second one has only one, rather long, subject and one main verb; it is more concise. These complex noun phrases are economical as they allow information to be compressed.

Explorative Task (ii)

Look at the breakdown of the noun phrase in the second sentence in the table below.

Determiner	Pre-modification	Noun	Post-modification
Brown's	important	research	into the causes of breast cancer

The sentences below contain a number of complex noun phrases, some of which have been highlighted. Add the highlighted noun phrases to the table above, and make a note of the structures that can be used in the different columns. Then compare with the table which follows.

1) Toxic chemical pollution of water resources mainly involves **agricultural and industrial contaminants**.
2) It is estimated that two-thirds of premature deaths in adults are traceable to **behaviour that started during teenage years**, especially (notably in lower-income countries) smoking, but also other risky activities (Hammond, 2011).
3) Tuberculosis is **a serious lower respiratory tract infection caused by *Mycobacterium tuberculosis***, an organism that is becoming more resistant to antibiotic treatment.
4) Because blood and lymph travel to all parts of the body, they are **good ways to spread infection**.
5) In the 19th century, Lord Kelvin proposed a thermodynamic method to specify temperature, based on the measurement of the quantity of **heat flowing between bodies** at different temperatures.

Typical noun phrase constructions			
Determiner	**Pre-modification**	**Noun**	**Post-modification**
articles (*a*; *the*) **demonstratives** (*this*; *that* etc.) **numbers and quantifiers** (*seven*; *several*; *every*; *some*; etc.) **possessives** (*my*; *his*; *Brown's*; etc.)	**adjectives** (e.g. *important*; *agricultural and industrial*; *serious*; *good*) **nouns** (e.g. *lower respiratory tract*)	**nouns used in a countable sense:** **singular** (e.g. *infection*) **plural** (e.g. *contaminants*; *ways*) **nouns used in an uncountable sense** (e.g. *research*; *behaviour*; *heat*)	**prepositional phrases** (e.g. *into the causes of breast cancer*) **relative clauses** (e.g. *that started during teenage years*) **participle clauses** (e.g. *caused by Mycobacterium*; *flowing between bodies*) **infinitive clauses** (e.g. *to spread infection*)

▨ Explorative Task (iii)

Long noun phrases occur frequently in academic scientific writing. Find two noun phrases of more than 10 words in the text.

> Besides their random nature, the tendency of material properties to vary spatially across the structure owing to the manufacture process or history effects can significantly influence structural behaviour. Random field theory (Ghanem and Spanos 2003, Liu *et al.* 1986, Missoum 2008) has been used in previous investigations to model material field uncertainty emanating from variability in the material microstructure in different locations of a structural component (Chen *et al.* 2010, Yin *et al.* 2009).
> (Salehghaffari *et al.*, 2013: 1027)

Study Box: Forming accurate noun phrases

1) Note that a countable noun must have a determiner if it is singular. One of the most common errors in non-native student writing is the omission of the article, or the use of a noun in the singular form when it should be in the plural, e.g.

They proposed using completely different method. ✗

They proposed using **a** completely different **method**. ✓

They proposed using completely different **methods**. ✓

Many nouns can be either countable or uncountable, depending on how they are used, e.g.

The drug was used to control **pain**.

The patient experienced **a** sharp **pain** in the abdomen.

Plural and uncountable nouns may or may not have a determiner, depending on whether or not they are **specified** in some way. Compare:

Plastic is a synthetic material.

The plastic used in this product is Bakelite.

This technique is widely used in **industry**.

This technique is widely used in **the car industry**.

Note that in the sentence below, *which* industry must be already understood because it has been previously specified in the text:

This technique is widely used in **the industry**.

Some terms always/usually occur with a definite article (*the UK*; *the US*; *the UN*; *the sun*; *the immune system*). Learn these and make a note of any others in your subject.

Remind yourself of these rules when you are using very common countable scientific words such as *method, system, level, technique, experiment* and *process*. Also, if you are

---

continued . . .

cont.

using a technical term from your subject repeatedly (*molecule*; *wire*; *super nova*; *dam*; *control system*), check in the dictionary to see if it is countable, and make sure you apply the rule each time – you should soon get into the habit and do it without thinking!

2) Always make sure the verb agrees with the subject of the sentence, even when it is separated from it, e.g.

The increasing demand for more sophisticated mobile devices are noted. ✗

The increasing **demand** for more sophisticated devices **is** noted. ✓

3) Remember that however long your noun phrase, it is still just the subject or object of your main verb (it could be replaced with one word like *it*). Therefore, you should never place a comma between the subject noun phrase and the verb, e.g.

Brown's important research into the causes of breast cancer, was funded by the British Medical Foundation. ✗

Brown's important research into the causes of breast cancer was funded by the British Medical Foundation. ✓

4) Post-modifying structures can themselves be long and complex, containing clauses or phrases, including more noun phrases, e.g.

behaviour [that started [during [teenage [years]]]]

Complex noun phrases often occur in academic scientific writing for good reason: they allow information to be compressed economically. However, they need to be constructed carefully. Moreover, they are not always the right choice: sometimes it is wiser to use a simpler **subject + verb** structure because this can often be clearer.

Practice (i)

Correct mistakes in the following sentences.

1) The proposal outlines flexible manufacturing control system suitable for chemical industries.
2) Scientist should work together to solve environmental problems.
3) The drug suppresses immune system.
4) The effect of pollution on marine mammals are examined in detail.
5) Galileo's greatest contribution to science, was his work in mechanics.

Practice (ii)

Combine these sentences together, using complex noun phrases.

1) Life expectancy in the developed world is increasing. This is partly due to improved nutrition and medical care.

The increase in _____

2) Many believe that alternative energy sources will solve our environmental problems. Some experts dispute this.

   The belief that _____

3) The modern diet comprises a great deal of processed foods. This is bound to have serious repercussions in terms of public health.

   The fact that _____

4) We may need more energy efficient data transfer in mobile devices. The paper assesses this.

   The paper _____

5) The amount of CO_2 in the atmosphere fluctuates depending on the season. This fluctuation occurs because, in the summer, the uptake of CO_2 by plants increases.

   The seasonal _____

Think about how you could use this technique to produce a simple **paraphrase** of original sources. ▶ **Chapter 7**

Common areas of difficulty in grammar and punctuation

A3.1 Common punctuation problems

A3.1.1 Apostrophes

The apostrophe denotes possession. Be careful to distinguish between singular and plural nouns:

- The bridge's structure was examined. (one bridge)
- The bridges' structures were examined. (several bridges)

A3.1.2 *it's* versus *its*

it's is the contracted form of *it is/has*:

- It's important to note the temperature.
- Note the colour of the liquid when it's cooled.

its is a possessive pronoun like *my* or *his*:

- When the liquid is heated, its colour changes.

> If you avoid contractions, you shouldn't need to use the apostrophe at all in this case.

A3.1.3 Hyphens in compound adjectives

Compound adjectives are usually hyphenated when they come before a noun, but not when they come after:

- an out-of-date technology
- a technology which is out of date
- a chemically-induced coma
- a coma that has been chemically induced

A3.1.4 Brackets

Brackets should be used sparingly as they can interrupt the flow of a text. If you do use them, be careful with punctuation. If the bracketed information is part of the sentence, it requires no specific punctuation, e.g.

- The data (collected over six months) revealed a noticeable decline in quality.

If the brackets contain a separate sentence, it should be punctuated as such:

- The data revealed a noticeable decline in quality. (All the data was collected over a six-month period.)

A3.2 Common grammar problems

A3.2.1 *fewer* versus *less*

fewer is used with countable nouns:

- fewer people/studies/elements

less is used with uncountable nouns:

- less time/research/energy

A3.2.2 *a number of*

The word *number* is singular and should, strictly speaking, be followed by a singular verb, e.g.

- A number of filter samples was collected.

However, often, when the noun closest to the verb is plural, it can seem more natural to use a plural verb, e.g.

- A number of filter samples were collected.

This 'principle of proximity' (Biber *et al.*, 1999: 190) is seen by many as acceptable, but it is best to avoid it in formal writing.

Do not use *amount* with plural nouns:

- A large amount of people. ✗
- A large number of people. ✓

A3.2.3 *data*

The word *data* is technically plural (*datum* being the singular), but it is often used in an uncountable sense, e.g.

- The data shows that temperatures have increased over the last decade.

A3.2.4 Word classes

Be careful to distinguish between nouns, verbs, adjectives and adverbs, e.g.

- Sulphur dioxide is presense in the environment. ✗
- Sulphur dioxide is **present** in the environment. ✓
- Computer programs are used to analysis samples. ✗
- Computer programs are used to **analyse** samples. ✓
- The unique characteristics of this substance, such as chemical stable, make it suitable for this application. ✗
- The unique characteristics of this substance, such as chemical **stability**, make it suitable for this application. ✓
- Nations worldwide have realised the important of reducing CO_2. ✗
- Nations worldwide have realised the **importance** of reducing CO_2. ✓

Be particularly careful with these common words:

- *emphasise/synthesise/analyse/hypothesise* (verbs)
- *emphasis/synthesis/analysis/hypothesis* (nouns)

Also, do not confuse *effect* (noun) and *affect* (verb):

- Carbon emissions have had a profound **effect** on the environment.
- Carbon emissions have profoundly **affected** the environment.

There is a verb *effect*, but it has a different meaning (to make happen, bring about), and is usually restricted to particular nouns like *change*.

- The government plans to **effect change** in the plastics industry.

A3.2.5 Sentence patterns

Many verbs occur in fixed sentence patterns:

- They succeeded in extraction graphene from graphite. ✗
- They **succeeded in** extract**ing** graphene from graphite. ✓
- They prevented the farmers plant crops in the area. ✗
- They **prevent**ed the farmers **from** plant**ing** crops in the area. ✓

Be careful to use the right sentence patterns with the following commonly used synonyms – note the use of prepositions and passive structures:

- Glass **consists of** sand plus a number of other substances.
- Glass **comprises** sand plus a number of other substances.
- Glass **is composed of** sand plus a number of other substances.
- Glass **is made up of** sand plus a number of other substances.

Note that different word classes may have different patterns:

- The study **lacks** rigour. (no preposition with verb)
- There is **a lack of** rigour in the study.

The phrase *to be lacking in* can also be used:

- The study **is lacking in** rigour.

A3.2.6 Prepositions

Mistakes commonly occur with the following prepositions:

- a **change in** temperature (a development)
- a **change of** government (a substitution)
- the **demand for** resources
- the **reason for** the change
- the **need for** change
- **in need of** reform
- the **rationale behind** the decision
- an **increase/decrease/rise/fall (of** 2%**) in** volume

A3.2.7 Irregular plurals

Make a note of irregular plurals common in scientific writing:

- analysis – analy**ses**
- antenna – antenn**ae**
- criterion – crit**eria**
- fungus – fung**i**
- phenomenon – phenom**ena**
- stimulus – stimul**i**
- stratum – strat**a**

Model texts

Model text 1: VLEs

Most universities **have** Virtual Learning Environments (VLEs) such as **B**lackboard and **M**oodle. **These** provide **an** online space for course modules where students can access **information** on course content, assessment, **and** further study. VLE**s** are also used for the electronic submission of assessed work, **which** enables lecturers to use software such as **T**urnitin to check for plagiarism in student**s'** work. A further function of VLEs is to provide a space for students **to** enter into discussion with each other. Whilst this would appear to be an excellent opportunity for all students to develop their idea**s** and understanding, and for non-native speakers to **practise** their language skills, it would seem that many are reluctant to engage in this type of activity. **T**he reasons **for** this remain unclear.

Model text 2: Paediatrics

Paediatrics is a branch of medicine that deals with the care of infants, children and adolescents up until the age of eighteen. Paediatric medicine differs from adult medicine in terms of physiology, and also in terms of individual legal status, in that children, unlike adults, are not able to make decisions for themselves.

Model text 3: Copper extraction

A number of techniques are used to extract copper. These include hydrometallurgy, solvent extraction, liquid–liquid electrochemistry and electrowinning. Each of these processes is described below, with the main focus of this project being liquid–liquid electrochemistry.

Model text 4: The discovery of graphene

Graphene is the thinnest, strongest material known to science. In addition, it is more effective than copper in conducting electricity. Geim and Konstantin, the two Manchester University researchers who discovered it, were subsequently awarded the 2011 Nobel Prize in Physics. They extracted graphene, which is comprised of a flat layer of carbon atoms tightly packed into a two-dimensional honeycomb structure (Figure 1), from the common material graphite, which is used in pencil leads. The method they used to extract the graphene was somewhat unusual: they applied the common, everyday product sticky tape to remove thin strips of carbon. Initially, they obtained flakes comprised of many layers. However, each time the process was repeated, the flakes became thinner.

Model text 5: Recycling

It is better to recycle products rather than disposing of them. There are two main reasons for this. Firstly, using recycled materials means that there is less need to extract raw materials from the earth. Secondly, it requires less energy to refine and process recycled materials than it does to refine and process natural resources.

Model text 6: Additives and chemicals

Many foods contain chemical additives. These take the form of preservatives, artificial sweeteners, artificial flavourings, and colouring agents, all of which are added by the manufacturer during production. Chemicals are also added to the food chain in agriculture through the widespread use of fertilisers and pesticides on crops, and the provision of antibiotics and supplements for livestock. The maximum allowed levels of these chemicals are strictly controlled by law. Therefore, quality control of raw materials and commercially-manufactured foodstuffs is essential to ensure that they are not contaminated beyond regulatory levels. One technique used to perform this quality control is *high-performance liquid chromatography (HPLC)*, which is a technique used to separate, identify and quantify components in a mixture. This is used in combination with a detection system, often *ultraviolet–visible (UV–VIS) spectroscopy*.

Model text 7: Nanotechnology

Nanotechnology can be defined as the understanding and control of materials at the nanoscale, i.e. at approximately 1 to 100 nanometers, where a nanometer is one billionth of a meter. The sheer scale of this can be understood if these measurements are applied to an average sheet of paper, which is approximately 100,000 nm in thickness.

The physical, chemical and biological properties of materials at the nanoscale are very different to those of atoms, molecules and materials in bulk.

The goal of nanotechnology is to exploit the unique properties of nanomaterials to enable novel applications. One promising area for these applications is medicine, where, for example, researchers are working at the nanoscale to develop new drug delivery methods.

Model text 8: Carbon emissions

Whilst acknowledging that carbon dioxide emissions reached a new high in 2012, the authors (PBL Netherlands Environmental Agency, 2013) note that the actual increase in global emissions for that year was the lowest for a decade. They conclude that this decrease reflects a shift towards greener energy use.

Or:

Carbon dioxide emissions reached a new high in 2012. However, the actual increase in global emissions for that year was the lowest for a decade (PBL Netherlands Environmental Agency, 2013). This decrease appears to reflect a shift towards greener energy use (PBL Netherlands Environmental Agency, 2013).

Model text 9: The balance

Atkins (2013) argues that the birth of the balance, which brought with it the possibility of weighing things precisely, constituted a truly significant development in science, and heralded the transition from alchemy to chemistry. He attaches great importance to the fact that the balance allowed 'meaningful' numbers to be attached to matter, bringing their study into the domain of the physical sciences, where they can be subjected to rigorous quantitative analysis.

Model text 10: Antibiotics

Antibiotics are a type of medication used to treat infections caused by bacteria, such as syphilis, tuberculosis, salmonella. They act by killing bacteria or slowing down their growth (Nordqvist, 2013).

The use of antibiotics began in 1929 with the discovery of penicillin. The decade following the Second World War saw the discovery and development of a number of important

continued . . .

cont.

antibiotics, and in the 1950s, described by Davies as 'the golden age of antibiotic discovery' (2006: 287), one half of the antibiotics in common use today were discovered. Combined with improved hygiene, antibiotics have been responsible for a huge reduction in global bacterial-related morbidity and mortality (Davies, 2006).

However, increased use and misuse of these drugs in humans and animals has led to a phenomenon known as 'antibiotic resistence' (US Food and Drug Administration; Davies, 2006). This resistance develops when harmful bacteria change, thus reducing or negating the effectiveness of the antibiotics previously used to treat them (US Food and Drug Administration). The emergence of 'superbugs', such as MRSAs, in hospitals and the wider community has raised serious concerns (McCracken and Phillips, 2012: 152).

Davies notes that much recent antibiotic research has been geared towards the discovery and design of new compounds which will be effective against resistant pathogens (2006). However, deep concerns remain. Britain's most senior medical advisor, Dame Sally Davies, has warned that the rise in antibiotic resistance could 'trigger a national emergency comparable to a catastrophic terrorist attack, pandemic flu or major coastal flooding' (in Sample, 2013). She has also pointed to the threat of what she calls an 'apocalyptic scenario' in the near future, when patients could die from routine infections after surgery because of a lack of effective antibiotics to treat them (in Sample, 2013).

The aim of this essay is to assess the extent of antibiotic resistance in today's society, and to explore the possible solutions to this problem.

References

Davies, J. (2006) Where have all the antibiotics gone? *Canadian Journal of Infectious Diseases and Medical Microbiology*, 17(5), 287–290.

McCracken, K. and D. Phillips (2012) *Global Health: An Introduction to Current and Future Trends*, Abingdon: Routledge.

Nordqvist, C. (2013) What are antibiotics? How do antibiotics work? *Medical News Today*, http://www.medicalnewstoday.com/articles/10278.php [accessed 1st December, 2013]

Sample, I. (2013) Antibiotic-resistant diseases pose 'apocalyptic' threat, top expert says, *Guardian*, 23rd January, http://www.theguardian.com/society/2013/jan/23/antibiotic-resistant-diseases-apocalyptic-threat [accessed 15th January, 2014]

U.S. Food and Drug Administration, *Combating antibiotic resistance*, http://www.fda.gov/downloads/ForConsumers/ConsumerUpdates/UCM143470.pdf [accessed 2nd December, 2013]

Model text 11: Equation

If a soap film is stretched across a frame with a moveable wire, the force required to hold the wire in place is:

$$F = 2yl \qquad\qquad (6.1)$$

where l is the length of the wire, y is the surface tension of the soap film/air interface and the factor 2 is introduced because the film has two surfaces.

Model text 12: GM foods

Genetically modified (GM) foods are becoming more widely available. Many see the increased production of GM crops as an important tool in the fight against world hunger. However, others are concerned by the possible effects of these foods on health.

Model text 13: Newton's three laws of motion

Newton's three laws of motion state that:

- a body continues in its state of rest of uniform motion in a straight line unless acted upon by an external force;
- the rate of change of momentum of a body is proportional to the applied force and takes place in the direction in which the force acts;
- for every action there is an equal and opposite reaction.

Answer Key

Chapter 2: The writing process

2.3 The importance of redrafting

▨ Explorative Task

Text B is easier to read for most people.

Which text	Text A student's first draft	Text B student's second draft
begins with a clear contextualisation of current developments in mobile systems?		✓
introduces the ideas in a logical, step-by-step fashion?		✓
has a clearer outline of what is to follow in the rest of the essay?		✓
has fewer grammatical errors and more natural expression? (*provide an overview* rather than *outline an overview*; *advice* should be uncountable; what's more, the tone of this is not very academic – you might *offer advice* to a friend but in papers like this, we usually *offer recommendations*)		✓

Chapter 3: Academic scientific style

3.1.1 Sentence length and text organisation

Explorative Task

1) Text B
2) Text A

3.1.2 Being concise

Practice (i) (suggested answers)

1) All the studies had limitations.
2) Scientists need to find solutions for these problems/Scientists need to solve these problems.
3) He compares the two systems.
4) In the conclusion, she reiterates the significance of the results.
5) Pollution is a global problem/Pollution is a problem throughout the world.

3.1.3 Being precise

Practice (suggested answers)

1) The regulations cover the use of fossil fuels such as oil and gas.
2) Buildings in the city are constructed of materials such as concrete and timber.
3) In terms of applications, this polymer is very versatile.
4) There are a number of factors affecting blood pressure.
5) There are many problems associated with obesity.

3.2.1 What is academic scientific writing?

Explorative Task

1) References

   Text A: academic textbook

   Housecroft, C. and E. Constable (2010) *Chemistry: An Introduction to Organic, Inorganic and Physical Chemistry*, (4th Edition), Harlow: Pearson Education.

   Text B: online article (news website)

   Rincon, P. (2011) *How sticky tape led to the Nobel Prize*, BBC, 5th October, http://www.bbc.co.uk/news/science-environment-11478645

Text C: academic textbook

Strelkauskas, A. , J. Strelkauskas and D. Moszyk-Strelkauskas (2010) *Microbiology: A Clinical Approach*, Abingdon: Garland Science.

Text D: popular science book

Hawking, S. and L. Mlodinov (2011) *The Grand Design: New Answers to the Ultimate Questions of Life*, New York: Bantam Books.

Text E: academic journal article

Arel, E. and A. Önalp (2012) Geotechnical properties of Adapazari silt, *Bulletin of Engineering Geology and the Environment*, 71, 709–720.

Text F: online article (popular science magazine)

Brooks, M. (2009) Rise of the robogeeks, *New Scientist*, 3rd March, http://www. newscientist.com/article/mg20126971.800-rise-of-the-robogeeks.html

Text G: academic journal article

Yamashita, H., H. Tsukayama and C. Sugishita (2002) Popularity of complementary medicine in Japan: a telephone survey, *Complementary Therapies in Medicine*, 10, 84–93.

Text H: academic journal article

Howard, S., J. Adams and M. White (2012) Nutritional content of supermarket ready meals and recipes by television chefs in the United Kingdom: cross sectional study, *BMJ* 2012; 345:e7607.

3.2.2 Common features of academic scientific texts

Explorative Task

1) a, b, f; 2) c, f, g; 3) examples of scientific/technical vocabulary: *proton, electron, neutron, mass, diabetes, heart disease, cancer, properties, outpatients, alternative therapy, acupuncture, chiropractic, deposited, low plasticity non-plastic silts, microorganisms, sewage*; 4) d; 5) b, e; 6) c, g

Practice (i)

1) *we're talking about, spawn, cyber-nerds*; 2) *it sounds like*; 3) *got*; 4) *bug-eyed aliens, starships*; 5) *reckons*; 6) *and* (at the start of a sentence); 7) use of dashes; 8) verb contraction, informal tone; 9) detailed biographical information in the text; 10) detailed biographical information in the text

Practice (ii)

1) a; 2) b; 3) b; 4) b; 5) a; 6) b; 7) a; 8) a

▨ **Practice (iii) (suggested answers)**

1) Initially, they obtained flakes consisting of many layers of graphene. However, each time the process was repeated, the flakes became thinner.
2) He believes that he has identified a key component of how humans develop mathematical ability.
3) This study aims to determine the cause of/what caused the structural damage.
4) A great deal of research has been conducted on the subject of runway friction.
5) Most thermometers are closed glass tubes containing liquids such as alcohol or mercury.
6) The solution was then heated to approximately 70°C.
7) The results of the analysis can be seen in Table 2.
8) Little is known about the proteins linked with RNA.
9) Eating disorders may cause individuals to feel tired and depressed.
10) There are three different types of volcano: active volcanoes, which erupt frequently; dormant volcanoes, which are temporarily inactive; extinct volcanoes, which are unlikely to erupt again.

Chapter 4: Sentence structure 1

4.1 Subject + verb structures

▨ **Explorative Task**

1) <u>Lime</u> (CaO) <u>is widely used</u> as an ingredient in mortars, plasters and masonry.
2) <u>One of the most noticeable trends over many decades</u> <u>has been</u> shifting patterns of health and especially the causes of morbidity (illness) and mortality (death).
3) <u>A motherboard</u> <u>is</u> the major circuit board inside a computer and <u>it</u> <u>holds</u> the processor, the computer bus, the main memory and many other vital components.
4) <u>Solar power</u> <u>is</u> one facet of renewable energy, with wind and geothermal being others.
5) Although quarantine <u>is</u> the oldest method of dealing with communicable diseases, <u>it</u> <u>is</u> now generally <u>used</u> only for very severe diseases, such as cholera and yellow fever.

4.2.1 Forming simple sentences

▨ **Explorative Task (i)**

1) Temperatures rose.
2) Temperatures rose <u>steadily</u>. (adverb, modifying the verb)
3) <u>Average</u> temperatures <u>in the south of the country</u> rose <u>steadily</u>. (adjective, pre-modifying the noun; prepositional phrase, post-modifying the noun)
4) <u>In the period from 2003 to 2013,</u> <u>average</u> temperatures <u>in the south of the country</u> rose <u>steadily</u>. (prepositional phrase, modifying the sentence)

▨ Explorative Task (ii)

1) It **is** undoubtedly true that computational simulations should not completely replace experimentation.
2) An ICT system is a set-up **consisting of/that consists of** hardware, software, data and the people who use these things.
3) Vitamin D is important for the absorption of calcium and phosphorus by the body. It is essential for the formation and health of bones, teeth and cartilage.

4.2.2 Compound and complex sentences

▨ Practice

1) Although the structure of the building was weakened, experts agreed that there was no danger of it collapsing. The structure of the building was weakened, but experts agreed that there was no danger of it collapsing.
2) The drug trial was abandoned because the side effects were considered to be too serious.
3) The panda was artificially inseminated and experts claimed that her hormone and behavioural signs indicated that she was carrying a foetus. However, changes in her behaviour suggest that she has lost the cub.

4.2.2.1 Forming compound sentences

▨ Practice

1) A poor diet can lead to obesity and cause a number of health problems.
2) The hurricane destroyed a number of buildings and caused major damage to trees.
3) The drug can be taken orally or injected.
4) The Internet has improved our lives in many ways but it has brought with it a number of problems.
5) Some patients respond well to therapy but others show little improvement.

4.2.2.2 Forming complex sentences with subordinating conjunctions

▨ Practice (i)

1) as; 2) whereas; 3) although; 4) in case; 5) as soon as

▨ Practice (ii) (original sentences)

1) While it remains the case that the brain as a whole has limited powers of repair, the potential use of stem cells offers new hope for future therapy for degenerative brain diseases. (*although* could also be used)

2) The stability of glass makes disposal difficult, as it will not readily break down.
3) The reasons for developing type 1 diabetes have not been identified, although some suggest interaction of dietary factors during pregnancy and early neonatal life. (*while* could also be used)
4) Whereas chemistry reaches down into physics for its explanations, it reaches upwards into biology for many of its extraordinary applications. (*while* could also be used)
5) It is sometimes necessary to acquire information regarding the cause of a ceramic fracture so that measures may be taken to reduce the likelihood of future incidents.

4.2.3.1 Participle clauses

Practice (original sentences)

1) prompting; 2) composed; 3) weighing; 4) using

4.2.3.2 Infinitive clauses of purpose

Practice (original sentences)

1) All structural concrete contains steel reinforcements in the form of bars or welded mesh to compensate for the low tensile strength of concrete.
2) We must understand the transmission mechanisms of infection so that we can interfere with those mechanisms to take effective public health measures.
3) Water is then added to dilute the acid to 20–30% and the mixture is again heated to 100°C for 1 hour.
4) Stemming from analytical chemistry is *forensic chemistry*, in which the techniques of analytical chemistry are used for legal purposes to track down suspects, and to analyse the scenes of crimes.
5) Aluminium–lithium alloys have been developed by the aircraft industry to reduce the weight and improve the performance of its aircraft.

4.2.3.3 *that*-clauses

Practice (original sentences)

1) Immunisation requires **that** we understand the immune mechanisms and **that** we design vaccines that will successfully stimulate protection.
2) One estimate suggests **that** 1.46 billion adults worldwide were overweight in 2008,[1] and projections suggest **that** by 2020 over 70% of adults in the United Kingdom and United States will be overweight.
3) It is popularly believed **that** the cells of wood are living cells, but this is certainly not the case.
4) Chemists take a great deal of interest in the rates of chemical reactions as there is little point knowing **that** they can, in principle, generate a substance in a reaction but **that** it would take a millennia to make a milligram.

5) Over time, it is becoming more apparent **that** the earth is virtually a closed system relative to its constituent materials and **that** its resources are finite.

4.2.4 Focus on relative clauses

Practice (i)

1) A computer virus is a program **that/which** can damage your computer.
2) Brisk walking is something (**that/which**) many doctors recommend to those **who/that**
are overweight.
3) A marine engineer is someone **who/that** works with underwater equipment and systems.
4) Vitamin C, (**which** is) also known as ascorbic acid, is required by the body for the growth
and repair of tissue.
5) Global warming leads to climate change, **which** will ultimately affect people all over the
world.

The relative pronoun can be omitted in 2). (See brackets above.)

4) can be reduced (see brackets above).

Practice (ii)

1) of; 2) in; 3) above; 4) at; 5) of, of

Practice (iii) (suggested answers)

1) Arsenic, which is an extremely toxic substance, is sometimes used as an insecticide.
2) The Royal Society, which was founded in 1660, is a self-governing fellowship of many of
the world's most distinguished scientists.
3) The disease has a number of symptoms, most of which can be controlled through medication.
4) The extent to which technology can help countries to develop is unclear.
5) Gravitational wave astronomy is an emerging new field of astronomy that/which aims to
use gravitational wave detectors to collect observational data about compact objects.
6) A crystal is a piece of matter whose boundaries are naturally formed planed surfaces.
7) It was Tim Berners-Lee who/that invented the Internet in 1989.
8) Fracking is a procedure whereby a solution is pumped into the earth to fracture rock and
access oil and gas.

Chapter 5: Sentence structure 2

5.1.1 Prepositional phrases

Practice

1) in spite of; 2) in addition to; 3) owing to; 4) throughout; 5) notwithstanding

5.1.2 Sentence connectors

Practice

1) consequently; 2) in contrast; 3) however; 4) subsequently; 5) on the contrary

5.1.3 Controlling syntax

Practice (i)

1) b; 2) d; 3) b, e; 4) a, f

Practice (ii) (suggested answers)

1) He studied computer science for a number of years. Subsequently, he did a PhD in software design.
2) Although it has been difficult for women to break into the field of science, they have been responsible for many important discoveries.
3) The water subsided quickly after the flood. However, there was still a huge amount of damage.
4) The patient was unable to sleep due to stress.
5) In addition to being very versatile, plastics are very durable.
6) While some antibacterial products kill bacteria, others only prevent them from multiplying.
7) This model of phone is very popular owing to its high degree of functionality.

Practice (iii) (some suggestions)

1)

In spite of/despite the drug's/its high success rate, it/the drug has not been adopted on a wide scale.

In spite of/despite the fact that the drug/it has a high success rate, it/the drug has not been adopted on a wide scale.

The drug has not been adopted on a wide scale in spite of/despite its high success rate.

The drug has not been adopted on a wide scale in spite of/despite the fact that it has a high success rate.

The drug has a high success rate. In spite of/despite this, it has not been adopted on a wide scale.

2)

The number of animal species found in these regions is declining as a result of the fact that/because huge areas of rainforest are being destroyed every day.

Huge areas of rainforest are being destroyed every day. Because of/As a result of this, the number of animal species found in these regions is declining.

3)

In addition to their many industrial applications, dyes are also widely used in medicine.

Dyes have many industrial applications. In addition, they are also widely used in medicine.

5.2 Focus on punctuation

Practice (original punctuation used)

1) Over the past two centuries, pollution has become one of the most pervasive and multi-faceted threats to human health.
2) In 1988, the Centers for Disease Control (CDC), concerned about the spread of HIV in hospitals, published a set of universal procedures requiring all medical facilities in the United States to conform to specific guidelines for patient care (Table 6.2).
3) Darwin was concerned with evolution, i.e. change over time, and he proposed a process, natural selection, that could bring about such change.
4) Chemical reactions normally occur in water, and water can also participate in reactions. (Comma could be omitted.)
5) If every individual in the world were to demand as much energy as the average person uses in North America, the global energy supply industries would require a five-fold increase in their use of primary energy sources.
6) After felling, a tree has to be processed in order to render the timber suitable for man's use.
7) The calculus of variations, which plays an important role in both pure and applied mathematics, dates from the time of Newton.
8) The computers which form the basis of those used today were mainly developed in the 1940s.
9) Scientists are able to identify parts of the brain that are specifically targeted by addictive drugs.
10) Einstein in his general theory of relativity (1915) proposed that the universe exists in four-dimensional space-time. (Commas could be used around 'in his general theory of relativity (1915)'.)
11) Aromatherapy users showed prominent characteristics: they were far more likely to be younger females, highly educated, who tend to live in urban areas.
12) The pH of the heartwood varies in different species of timber, but is generally about 4.5 to 5.5; however, in some timbers such as eucalypt, oak, and western red cedar, the pH of the heartwood can be as low as 3.0. (Commas can be omitted before 'but' and 'and'.)

5.3 Lists and parallel structures

Practice (suggested answers)

1) There are three types of rock: igneous, sedimentary and metamorphic.
2) Blood vessels can be classified into three types: arteries, which carry blood away from the heart; capillaries, which connect arteries to veins; and veins, which carry blood back to the heart.

3) Deciduous trees lose their leaves seasonally; evergreen trees maintain their green foliage all year round.

4) Western experts refer to four types of taste: sweet, salty, sour and bitter; eastern experts also include umami.

5) The trunk of a tree has three physical functions to perform: firstly, it must support the crown, a region responsible for the production not only of food, but also of seed; secondly, it must conduct the mineral solutions absorbed by the roots upwards to the crown; and thirdly it must store manufactured food (carbohydrates) until required. (Domone and Illstone, 2010: 405)

Chapter 6: Paragraph development: the flow of ideas

6.1.1 Given versus new information

Explorative Task

Food additives are substances that are added to food to improve shelf-life, appearance and flavour. Two **substances** which have been added to food for centuries are vinegar and salt. Many **more additives**, both natural and artificial, are now used in modern food processing.

Geckos, harmless tropical lizards, are extremely fascinating and extraordinary animals. **They** have very sticky feet that cling to virtually any surface. **This characteristic** makes it possible for them to rapidly run up vertical walls and along the undersides of horizontal surfaces. **In fact**, a gecko can support its body mass with a single toe! The secret to **this remarkable ability** is the presence of an extremely large number of microscopically small hairs on each of their toe pads. When **these hairs** come into contact with a surface, weak forces of attraction (i.e. van der Waals forces) are established between hair molecules and molecules on the surface. The fact that **these hairs** are so small and so numerous explains why the gecko grips surfaces so tightly. To release **its grip, the gecko** simply curls up its toes, and peels **the hairs** away from **the surface**.

Practice (suggested answers)

1) Cereals are one of the most important staple foods. The major cereals of the world are wheat, rye, barley, oats, maize, rice, millet and sorghum.

2) Beer is a fermented alcoholic beverage. The main ingredients of beer are malt and hops.

3) A ligament is a resilient but flexible band of tissue that holds two or more bones together at a moveable joint. Ligaments restrain movement of bones at a joint and are therefore important in preventing dislocation.

4) Chalk is a very fine-grained white rock composed of the fossilised skeletal remains of marine plankton and consisting largely of calcium carbonate. Chalk is used to make toothpaste and cosmetics. It is not the same thing as blackboard 'chalk', which is actually made from calcium sulphate.

6.1.2 General and specific

Explorative Task

Text A: 1) b; 2) a; 3) c
Text B: 1) e; 2) a; 3) c; 4) d; 5) b
Text C: 1) b; 2) a; 3) f; 4) c; 5) e; 6) d

Practice (original texts)

Text A: 1) c; 2) a; 3) e; 4) d; 5) b
Text B: 1) d; 2) e; 3) b; 4) c; 5) f; 6) a; 7) h; 8) g

6.2 Cohesive devices

Explorative Task

2) 20, 21 ellipsis; 22, 25, 26 repetition; 23, 30 use of *this/that* + noun to refer back; 24 linking expression; 27, 28, 29 pronouns

Practice (i) (original text)

1) its; 2) it; 3) its; 4) this; 5) which

Practice (ii) (original text)

1) they; 2) omega-3; 3) it; 4) which; 5) they; 6) omega-3; 7) she; 8) omega-3

Practice (iii) (original text)

1) these new materials; 2) furthermore; 3) at this point; 4) this knowledge; 5) thus; 6) these; 7) for example

6.3 Focus on punctuation

Practice (original text and punctuation)

An animal's survival prospects are greatly improved if the animal alters its behaviour according to its experience. Learning increases its chances of obtaining food, avoiding predators, and adjusting to other often unpredictable changes in its environment. The importance of learning in the development of behaviour was stressed particularly by US experimental psychologists, such as John B. Watson (1878–1958) and B. F. Skinner (1904–90), who studied animals under carefully controlled laboratory conditions. They demonstrated how rats and pigeons could be trained, or 'conditioned', by exposing them to stimuli in the form of food rewards or electric shocks. This work was criticised by others, notably the ethologists, who preferred to observe animals in their natural surroundings and who stressed the importance of inborn mechanisms, such as instinct, in behavioural development. A synthesis between these two once-conflicting approaches has been achieved: learning is regarded as a vital aspect of an animal's development, occurring in response to stimuli in the animal's environment, but within the constraints set by the animal's genes. Hence young animals are receptive to a wide range of stimuli but are genetically predisposed to respond to those that are more significant.

Chapter 7: Referring to sources: paraphrase, referencing, criticality and the issue of plagiarism

Explorative Task

- If I have lots of references to other people's work, it won't be *my* work, it won't be original. WRONG ▶ 7.2
- I can use other people's words as long as I give a reference. WRONG ▶ 7.2
- If I use my own words to explain someone else's work, I don't need to give a reference. WRONG ▶ 7.1
- I can paraphrase by replacing some words with synonyms. WRONG ▶ 7.1
- I must change every word in a source I am using. WRONG ▶ 7.1

7.1.2 Good reasons to use your own words

Explorative Task (ii)

Which text	Text A	Text B	Text C
uses original sentence structure and phrasing, just retaining technical terms?	✗	✓	✓
selects particular information?	✗	✓	✓
adds some information?	✗	✓	✓
is clearly referenced?	✗	✗	✓
is an acceptable paraphrase?	✗	✗	✓

7.1.3 Good reasons *not* to use your own words

Explorative Task

Renewable energy; the 1973 OPEC oil embargo; fossil fuels; photosynthesis in plants; chlorophyll; absorb solar radiation; charge separation

7.2 Adopting good academic practice: referencing and criticality

Explorative Task (ii)

2)
   a) reference to sources; use of phrases which indicate that they have identified a general consensus in the literature (*is increasingly recognised*), and assessed the credibility of the evidence (*have shown; have identified*); assertion in the final sentence that they have identified a gap in the research
   b) text comprehensively referenced; expression **multiple** *studies*
   c) The last sentence indicates their own assessment of the research in the field and their identification of a gap in the research.
   d) Yes – they have done a wide literature survey, assessed the studies critically and used the findings to support their argument. It is a **reasoned** argument.

Explorative Task (iii)

1)
   a) demonstrate that; b) conclude that; c) note that; d) advocate

2)
   a) found that; b) supermarket ready meals; c) acknowledging; d) supermarkets; e) positive

7.3 Strategies for paraphrase and summary

Practice (i): Paraphrasing scientific facts

1) control; 2) 1–100; 3) meter; 4) thickness; 5) properties; 6) chemical; 7) bulk; 8) novel/new; 9) DNA

Chapter 8: Textual development: structure, coherence, argument and critical thinking

8.1 Structure and coherence

Explorative Task

1)
   A

   i) d; ii) c; iii) b; iv) a; v) g; vi) e; vii) f

   B

   i) b; ii) d; iii) c; iv) a; v) f; vi) e

2)

   a) Method; b) Abstract; c) Introduction; d) Results and discussion; e) Conclusion

3)   Abstract – present (ref to general research)/past (ref to experiment); Method – past;
     Results and discussion – present (ref to results/data)/past (discussion); Conclusion –
     present (ref to paper in general)/past (ref to results)
4)   past simple passive
5)   *first*; *then*; *after cooling*; *after drying*; *the resulting material*; *the treated material*
6)   Results: *Table III shows*; *slightly increases when* Discussion: *this was possible because of*;
     that may cause
7)   *The results from this study demonstrated that*
8)   *higher*; *while*; *both*
9)   Introduction – specifies problem behind the investigation; Conclusion – summarises
     findings/gives implications of the findings

8.1.1 Focus on Introductions and Conclusions

Explorative Task

1)

   2.   The Mechanism of Fatigue
   2.2 Fatigue Crack Propagation
   2.3 Final Fracture
   3.1 Surface Roughness
   3.3 The Effects of Treatments and Coatings

2)
opening statement

   *Fatigue, the tendency of a material, such as metal, to break after being subjected to cyclic
   loading, has been the subject of research for more than 150 years.*

background/context

   paragraphs 2 and 3

definitions of key terms

   *Fatigue, the tendency of a material, such as metal, to break after being subjected to cyclic
   loading*

rationale behind the investigation

   A complete solution to the problem of fatigue has not yet been discovered [1].

purpose of the project

   *The objective of this project is to examine the process of fatigue failure in carbon steel,
   with a view to assessing the role of coatings in combatting this problem.*

outline of the project structure

   *It will begin by outlining the mechanism of fatigue. It will then discuss the source of
   fatigue, and ways of preventing it, with particular focus on the use of coatings.*

8.1.2 Describing methodology

Practice (original text)

1)

a) focussed; b) was observed; c) had; d) spent; e) were released; f) were fed

2)

a) to; b) at, of; c) with; d) from; e) to

3)

a) The material was cut was into 2 cm strips.
b) After cooling, the solution was mixed with 10 ml of water.
c) The alarm system was installed throughout the building and then monitored for six months.
d) To prevent corrosion, the metal was treated with a coating.
e) Post-natal surveys were conducted using email and focus groups.

8.1.3 Describing and discussing results

Practice

1)

a) found no evidence of; b) were significantly higher/were significantly higher; c) are comparable; d) It is unlikely that; e) several strengths; f) beyond the scope of; g) there is no evidence to support

2)

specific findings based on data,	b
general findings	c
the implications of the findings,	g
the strengths of the study	e
limitations of the study	f
the need for further research	f

8.2 Maintaining coherence

Explorative Task

2)

1, definition; 2. history; 3, basic principle; 4, main techniques; 5, technical analysis of a key point

5) The word 'masonry' is repeated, which guides the reader through the text reminding them that we are exploring a new aspect of this topic in each paragraph.

6) **in this wider sense** – refers directly to the more general of the two definitions given previously; paragraphs 3 and 4 are linked by the notion of **stability**; the list of techniques is referred back to by **type 4 structures**; **all other types**; paragraph 5 refers directly to the list of

techniques in paragraph 4 (**these descriptions**) and is explicit about why these techniques have been described, i.e. to show that it is the physical construction of most masonry that gives it its stability, rather than the adhesive character of the mortar.

7) These descriptions are given **to emphasise that**; although modern mortars **do** have an adhesive role much of the strength still derives from mass and friction between interlocking shapes; **it is important to remember this** in design.

Practice

2)

1, b; 2, c; 3, a

3) Paragraph 1 begins with a clear topic sentence giving relevance and significance to the subject; the first sentence in paragraph 2 is structured to give focus to the last two words (**not** the physical casualties **but** the *psychological impact*); in the first sentence of paragraph 3, the phrase '**more importantly**' gives a clear focus for the reader.

4)

a) Perhaps **more importantly**, the initial symptoms may not lead health care providers to suspect bioterrorism.
i.e. more importantly than the psychological and social implications mentioned in paragraph 2

5)

a) Bioweapons constitute a real threat in today's society as many people have access to them.
b) One reason bioweapons are so dangerous is that they not only cause physical damage, but can have an immense psychological impact on communities.
c) Moreover, the effects of bioweapons can be difficult to deal with because their presence can be difficult to detect, thus delaying early diagnosis and increasing exposure.

8.3 Building an argument

Explorative Task (i)

1)

Claim	Support (the reasons for this)	Source (of evidence)
Elephants find it difficult to keep cool.	They have an enormous body mass, small surface-to-volume ratio and a lack of sweat glands.	(Spearman, 1970; Hiley, 1975; Wright, 1984; Mariappa, 1986)
The ears of an elephant are the most important organ for regulating its temperature.	They have a large surface-to-volume ratio and an extensive and prominent vascular supply, which makes the ears the optimal organ for heat dissipation.	(Wright, 1984)

2) owing to; which predestines

3)

Statement	Premise (assumed fact behind the claim)	Support (statistical evidence)	Source
Overweight and obesity are major threats to public health globally.	Large numbers of people are over-weight/obese.	One estimate suggests that 1.46 billion adults worldwide were overweight in 2008,[1] and projections suggest that by 2020 over 70% of adults in the United Kingdom and United States will be overweight.[2]	Two articles from a peer-reviewed medical journal *The Lancet*.

4)

Statement	Support (examples)
Infectious diseases remain a major threat to global animal and human health.	2002 Foot and Mouth Disease outbreak in the UK; 2003 global epidemic of SARS; threat of an influenza pandemic

Explorative Task (ii)

3)
    a) a <u>well-known</u> material with <u>various</u> applications on an <u>industrial scale</u>
    b) Activated carbons that are <u>currently</u> commercially available are <u>expensive</u>, <u>however</u>
    c) <u>Therefore</u>, the search for alternative low-cost bio-based materials, as well as the appropriate processes for the preparation of activated carbons from these abundant resources, <u>has become necessary</u>
    d) the search for alternative <u>low-cost bio-based materials</u>, as well as the appropriate processes for the preparation of activated carbons from these abundant resources, has become necessary

4) processes for the preparation of activated carbons (paragraph 1)/methods for preparing the activated carbons (paragraph 2)

5)
    a) 4
    b) 1, physical activation; 2, chemical preparation; 3, combination of chemical and physical activation; 4, other factors affecting characteristics of activated material
    c) the methods for preparing the activated carbons can be divided into two categories: physical activation and chemical activation.

        In physical activation …/In chemical activation …
        combinations of chemical activation followed by physical activation methods …
        activated carbons prepared using different types of raw materials, activation processes, types of precursors, or compositions and process conditions result in different textural and functional characteristics

6) With an explanation of how rice can be used in the preparation of activated carbons. The preceding paragraphs prepare for this by indicating the need for 'alternative low-cost bio-materials' and the possibilities for combinations of raw materials and preparation methods.

7) 'The characteristics of activated carbons derived from deoiled rice bran residues make rice a **promising** raw material for the **production** of activated carbon.'

8)

a) Activated carbon is a useful material so we need to produce more of it.
b) As it is expensive to produce, we need to find ways of lowering the cost of production.
c) Using low-cost bio-based materials would help reduce the cost of production, so rice, as a relatively cheap biological product, might be a good alternative.
d) Different processes work differently with different materials, affecting the characteristics of the finished product. For this reason, it will be interesting to see how rice reacts.
e) Rice is abundant in Thailand. Therefore, if it turns out to be suitable for the production of deactivated carbon, there will be a plentiful supply of raw material.

9) By in-depth referencing to authoritative sources.

Chapter 9: Academic and scientific conventions

9.1 Referencing conventions

Explorative Task (ii)

1)

A: Harvard
B: Vancouver

5)

a) Atkins, P. (2013) *What Is Chemistry?* Oxford: Oxford University Press.
b) Housecroft, C. and E. Constable (2010) *Chemistry: An Introduction to Organic, Inorganic and Physical Chemistry*, (4th Edition), Harlow: Pearson Education.
c) Dinwoodie, J. (2010) Timber, in P. Domone and J. Illston (2010) (eds) *Construction Materials: Their Nature and Behaviour*, Abingdon: Spon Press, 403–506.
d) Davies, J. (2006) Where have all the antibiotics gone? *Canadian Journal of Infectious Diseases and Medical Microbiology*, 17(5), 287–290.
e) Rincon, P. (2011) *How sticky tape led to the Nobel Prize*, BBC, 5th October, http://www.bbc.co.uk/news/science-environment-11478645 [accessed 4th March, 2013].
f) *Royal Society*, http://royalsociety.org [accessed 20th November, 2012].

9.2 Incorporating quotation

Practice (suggested answers)

1) The *Oxford Dictionary of Science* defines polymers as 'substances that have macromolecules composed of many repeating units (known as "mers")' (2005: 648).

2) The structure of an atom is comprised of 'a nucleus surrounded by a cloud of atoms' (Atkins, 2013: 17).
3) According to Smolin, 'the desire to comprehend nature has been framed by the Platonic ideal that the world is a reflection of some perfect mathematical form' (in Dawkins, 2009: 363).
4) Davies describes the period from 1950 to 1960 as 'the golden age of antibiotic discovery' (2006: 287).

9.3 Tables and figures

Practice (i)

1) illustrated; 2) shows; 3) seen; 4) presents; 5) demonstrated; 6) compares

Practice (ii)

1) doubled; declined

9.4 Equations

Explorative Task

2)
A: where M is the metal and O is the oxygen
B: In reaction 1.42, O_2 is the *oxidising agent* and in reaction 1.43, H_2 is the *reducing agent*.

9.5 Units of measurement

Practice

1) Temperatures may reach 40°C. (capital C)
2) The wire measured 2 mm in diameter. (space between number and unit)
3) The machine weighs 44 kg. (no capitals)
4) Measure 2 l of water. (no s for plural)
5) 2 g of solution were added to every m^3 of water. (superscript 3)

9.6 Acronyms and abbreviations

Explorative Task (i)

Rule for Acronym Use

When mentioning a term for the first time, use <u>the full term</u> and put <u>the acronym</u> in brackets afterwards. After this, always use <u>the acronym</u>. (N.B. Do not keep switching from one to the other in a random fashion – it is very distracting for the reader.)

▓ **Explorative Task (ii)**

	Abbreviation	**Derivation**	**Meaning**
sentence 1	e.g.	*exempli gratia*	for example
sentence 2	i.e.	*id est*	that is to say
sentence 3	cf.	*confer*	compare and contrast*
sentence 4	N.B.	*nota bene*	note

*Sometimes used to mean 'see', although this usage is not accepted as correct by many

9.8 UK versus US spelling

A: UK
B: US

Both *ise* and *ize* are used in UK spelling – but be consistent.

Appendix 1: Verb forms and patterns

A1.1 Verb forms

▓ **Practice (i)**

1) boils; 2) is found; 3) was invented; 4) have been developed; 5) have been shown; 6) has been carried out

▓ **Practice (ii)**

1) rises, sets; 2) are becoming; 3) discovered, was expanding, had been done; 4) have made; 5) was added

▓ **Practice (iii)**

1) reaches; 2) is; 3) implemented, would fall; 4) had been vaccinated, would/could have been prevented

▓ **Practice (iv): Describing processes**

1) relies; 2) is heated; 3) pumped; 4) traps; 5) carry; 6) is insulated

A1.2 Verb patterns

Practice

1) Water pressure causes the wheel to turn.
2) Continued use of fossil fuels may give rise to climate change.
3) The safety measures introduced last year have led to a decrease in accidents.
4) Better technology in the future should result in more efficient energy production.
5) Dirty water could result in sickness, which could, in turn, trigger a national health crisis.

Appendix 2: Complex noun phrases

Explorative Task (iii)

the tendency of material properties to vary spatially across the structure owing to the manufacture process or history effects (19 words)
material field uncertainty emanating from variability in the material microstructure in different locations of a structural component (17 words)

Practice (i)

1) The proposal outlines a flexible manufacturing control system suitable for chemical industries.
2) Scientists should work together to solve environmental problems.
3) The drug suppresses the immune system.
4) The effect of pollution on marine mammals is examined in detail.
5) Galileo's greatest contribution to science was his work in mechanics.

Practice (ii) (suggested answers)

1) The increase in life expectancy in the developed world is partly due to improved nutrition and medical care.
2) The belief that alternative energy sources will solve our environmental problems is disputed by some experts.
3) The fact that the modern diet comprises a great deal of processed foods is bound to have repercussions in terms of public health.
4) The paper assesses the possible need for more efficient data transfer in mobile devices.
5) The seasonal fluctuation in the amount of CO_2 in the atmosphere occurs because of the increase in the uptake of CO_2 by plants in summer.

Bibliography

Academic Phrasebank, http://www.phrasebank.manchester.ac.uk/

Badge J. and J. Scott (2009) Dealing with plagiarism in the digital age. *Higher Education Academy EvidenceNet*, http://evidencenet.pbworks.com/w/page/19383480/Dealing%20with%20 plagiarism%20in%20the%20digital%20age

Biber, D., S. Johansson, G. Leech, S. Conrad and E. Finegan (1999) *Longman Grammar of Spoken and Written English*, Harlow: Pearson Education.

Dreifus, C. (1999) A conversation with Stephen Jay Gould, *New York Times*, 21st December, http://www.nytimes.com/1999/12/21/science/conversation-with-stephen-jay-gould-primordial-beasts-creationists-mighty.html?pagewanted=all&src=pm

Halliday, M. and H. Rugaiya (1976) *Cohesion in English*, Harlow: Pearson Education.

International System of Units (2006) Bureau International des Poids et Mesures (8th edition), http://www.bipm.org/utils/common/pdf/si_brochure_8_en.pdf

Medawar, P., Science and Literature (1974), in R. Dawkins (ed.) (2008) *The Oxford Book of Modern Science Writing*, Oxford: Oxford University Press.

Peck, J. and M. Coyle (2012) *Write It Right: The Secrets of Effective Writing*, (2nd edition), New York: Palgrave Macmillan.

Royal Society of Chemistry, http://www.rsc.org/

Woodford, P. (1967) Sounder thinking through clearer writing, *Science*, 156(3776), 743–745.

Sources of authentic example texts and sentences

Arel, E. and A. Önalp (2012) Geotechnical properties of Adapazari silt, *Bulletin of Engineering Geology and the Environment*, 71, 709–720.

Atkins, P. (2013) *What Is Chemistry?* Oxford: Oxford University Press.

Biber, D., S. Johansson, G. Leech, S. Conrad and E. Finegan (1999) *Longman Grammar of Spoken and Written English*, Harlow: Pearson Education.

Brooks, M. (2009) Rise of the robogeeks, *New Scientist*, 3rd March, http://www.newscientist.com/article/mg20126971.800-rise-of-the-robogeeks.html

Brown, N., D. Collison, R. Edge, E. Fitzgerald, P. Low, M. Helliwell, Y. Ta and M. Whiteley (2010) Metal-stabilised diynyl radicals, *Chem. Commun.*, 46, 2253–2255.

Callister, W. (2007) *Materials Science and Engineering: An Introduction*, New York: John Wiley and Sons.

Climatic Research Unit, University of East Anglia, http://www.cru.uea.ac.uk/

Danny, H., W. Li and S. L. Wong (2007) Daylighting and energy implications due to shading effects from nearby buildings, *Applied Energy*, 84, 1199–1209.

Dangour, A., K. Sakhi, A. Hayter, E. Allen, K. Lock and R. Uauy (2009) Nutritional quality of organic foods: a systematic review, *The American Society for Nutrition*, 10.3945/ajcn.2009.28041, http://ajcn.nutrition.org/content/early/2009/07/29/ajcn.2009.28041.full.pdf+html

Davies, J. (2006) Where have all the antibiotics gone? *Canadian Journal of Infectious Diseases and Medical Microbiology*, 17(5), 287–290.

Dawkins, R. (2008) (ed.) *The Oxford Book of Modern Science Writing*, Oxford: Oxford University Press.

Domone, P. and J. Illston (2010) (eds) *Construction Materials: Their Nature and Behaviour*, Abingdon: Spon Press.

Fgrup, *Bioethanol production*, http://fgrup.net/eng/production

Hawking, S. and L. Mlodinov (2011) *The Grand Design: New Answers to the Ultimate Questions of Life*, New York: Bantam Books.

High Energy Astrophysics Science Archive Research Centre, *Supernova*, http://heasarc.gsfc.nasa.gov/docs/snr.html

Housecroft, C. and E. Constable (2010) *Chemistry: An Introduction to Organic, Inorganic and Physical Chemistry*, (4th Edition), Harlow: Pearson Education.

Howard, S., J. Adams and M. White (2012) Nutritional content of supermarket ready meals and recipes by television chefs in the United Kingdom: cross sectional study, *BMJ*, 2012; 345:e7607, http://www.bmj.com/content/345/bmj.e7607

Huber, M., J. Knottnerus, L. Green, H. van der Horst, A. Jadad, D. Kromhout, B. Leonard, K. Lorig, M. Loureiro, J. van der Meek, P. Schnabel, R. Smith, C. van Weel and H. Smid (2011) How should we define health? *BMJ*, 2011; 345:d4163, http://www.bmj.com/content/343/bmj.d4163.pdf%2Bhtml

Kuno, M. (2012) *Introductory Nanoscience: Physical and Chemical Concepts*, Abingdon: Garland Science.

Maffeis, T. *Nanotechnology*, Royal Society, http://royalsociety.org/news/metro/nanotechnology/

McCracken, K. and D. Phillips (2012) *Global Health: An Introduction to Current and Future Trends*, Abingdon: Routledge.

Moller-Levet, C., S. Archer, G. Bucca, E. Laing, A. Slak, R. Kabiljo, J. Lo, N. Santhi, M. Schantz, C. Smith and D. Dijk (2013) Effects of insufficient sleep on circadian rhythmicity and expression amplitude of the human blood transcriptome, *Proceedings of the National Academy of Sciences of the United States of America*, http://www.pnas.org/content/early/2013/02/20/1217154110.full.pdf+html

Nanotechnology Initiative, *What is nanotechnology?* http://www.nano.gov/html/facts/whatisnano.html

Niticharoenwong, B., A. Shotipruk, O. Mekasuwandumrong, J. Panpranot and B. Jongsomjit (2013) Characteristics of activated carbons derived from deoiled rice bran residues, *Chem. Eng. Comm.*, 200, 1309–1321.

Nordqvist, C. (2013) What are antibiotics? How do antibiotics work? *Medical News Today*, http://www.medicalnewstoday.com/articles/10278.php

Okasha, S. (2002) *Philosophy of Science*, Oxford: Oxford University Press.

OpenLearn, *Addiction and neural aging*, http://www.open.edu/openlearn/ocw/mod/oucontent/view.php?id=2582&printable=1#section4.5

OpenLearn, *Evolution by natural selection*, http://www.open.ac.uk/StudentWeb/s292/LTIC/Downloads/Extract1.htm

OpenLearn, *LabSpace, Computers and computer systems*, http://labspace.open.ac.uk/mod/resource/view.php?id=438847

OpenLearn, *Studying mammals: A winning design*, http://www.open.edu/openlearn/nature-environment/natural-history/studying-mammals-winning-design/content-section-0

OpenLearn, *Studying mammals: Return to water*, http://www.open.edu/openlearn/nature-environment/natural-history/studying-mammals-return-the-water/content-section-0

Open University, *Calculus of variations and advanced calculus*, http://www3.open.ac.uk/study/postgraduate/course/m820.htm

Oxford Dictionary of Science (2005) Oxford: Oxford University Press.

Physicsis.com, *Temperature*, http://www.physicsis.com/temperature.htm

PBL Netherlands Environmental Assessment Agency (2013) *Trends in global CO_2 emissions: 2013 report*, http://www.pbl.nl/en/publications/trends-in-global-co2-emissions-2013-report

Rincon, P. (2011) *How sticky tape led to the Nobel Prize*, BBC, 5th October, http://www.bbc.co.uk/news/science-environment-11478645

Royal Society, http://royalsociety.org

Rubin, J. (2006) Are some people sensitive to mobile phone signals? *BMJ*, 2006, 15; 332(7546):886–91, http://www.bmj.com/content/332/7546/886.pdf%2Bhtml

Salehghaffari, S., M. Rais-Rohani, E. Marin and D. Bammann (2013) Optimisation of structures under material parameter uncertainty using evidence theory, *Engineering Optimisation*, 45(9), 1027–1041.

Sample, I. (2013) Antibiotic-resistant diseases pose 'apocalyptic' threat, top expert says, *Guardian*, 23rd January, http://www.theguardian.com/society/2013/jan/23/antibiotic-resistant-diseases-apocalyptic-threat

Smith, M. (2013) The Human Fertilisation and Embryology Act 2008: restrictions on the creation of 'saviour siblings' and the relevance of the harm principle, *New Genetics and Society*, 32(2), 154–170.

Strelkauskas, A. , J. Strelkauskas and D. Moszyk-Strelkauskas (2010) *Microbiology: A Clinical Approach*, Abingdon: Garland Science.

Unilife (2013) The University of Manchester, 10(6).

U.S. Food and Drug Administration, *Combating antibiotic resistance*, http://www.fda.gov/downloads/ForConsumers/ConsumerUpdates/UCM143470.pdf

Weissenbock, N., C. Weiss, H. Schwammer and H. Kratochvil (2010) Thermal windows on the body surface of African elephants (*Loxodonta africana*) studied by infrared thermography, *Journal of Thermal Biology*, 35, 182–188.

World Health Organization, *World report on road traffic injury prevention* (2004) Geneva, Figure 2.1, page 34, http://whqlibdoc.who.int/publications/2004/9241562609.pdf?ua=1, [last accessed 27th February, 2014]

World Steel Association (2009) *Statistics Archive* http://world.steel.org, [last accessed 27th February, 2014]

Yamashita, H., H. Tsukayama and C. Sugishita (2002) Popularity of complementary medicine in Japan: a telephone survey, *Complementary Therapies in Medicine*, 10, 84–93.

Example sentences cited

4.1

Domone and Illston (2010) p. 133, p. 253; Strelkauskas *et al.* (2010) p. 19, p. 54, p.121; OpenLearn, *Computers and computer systems*; Kuno (2012) p. 420; Atkins (2013) p. 17

4.2.2

McCracken and Philips (2012) p. 157

4.2.2.1

McCracken and Philips (2012) p. 165; Domone and Illston (2010) p. 515

4.2.2.2

OpenLearn, Addiction and neural aging; Domone and Illston (2010) p. 528; McCracken and Philips (2012) p.167; Atkins (2013) p. 6; Strelkauskas *et al.* (2010) p. 444

4.2.3.1

Howard et al. (2012); OpenLearn, *Addiction and neural aging*; Okasha (2002) p. 77; Atkins (2013) p. 2; Strelkauskas *et al.* (2010) p. 699

4.2.3.2

Domone and Illston (2010) p. 189; *Egrup*; Atkins (2013) p. 12; Strelkauskas *et al.* (2010) p. 108; Housecroft *et al.* (2010) p. 590

4.2.3.2

Atkins (2013) p. 33, p. 39; Howard *et al.*; Domone and Illston (2010) p. 407; Strelkauskas *et al.* (2010) p. 195

4.2.4

Howard et al.; Yamashita et al. (2002) p. 86; Domone and Illston (2010) p. 516, p. 546; Strelkauskas *et al.* (2010) p. 11; Biber *et al.* (1999) p. 618

5.2

Dawkins (2008) p. 363, p. 88, p. 41, p. 34, p. 60; McCracken and Philips (2012) p. 232, p. 108; OpenLearn, *Evolution by natural selection*; Domone and Illston (2010) p. 487, p. 414; Open-Learn, *Calculus of variation and advanced calculus*; OpenLearn, *Computers and computer systems*; Physicsis.com; Yamashita *et al.* (2002) p. 91

5.3

OpenLearn, *Studying mammals: Return to water*; Oxford Dictionary of Science (2005) p. 127, p. 805, p. 145–146

8.4

OpenLearn, *Studying mammals: A winning design*; Domone and Illston (2010) p. 175; Kuno (2012) p. 2

9.2

Yamishita *et al.*, (2002) p. 84; Smith (2013) p. 162; *Oxford Dictionary of Science* (2005) p. 648; Atkins (2013) p. 17; Smolin, in Dawkins (2009) p. 363; Davies (2006) p. 287

9.4

Domone and Illston (2010) p. 63, p. 45; Housecroft and Constable (2010) p. 43.

9.7

Domone and Illston (2010) p. 312, p. 247; McCracken and Philips (2012) p. ; Weissenbock *et al.* (2010) p. 183.

Appendix 2

McCracken and Philips (2012) p. 232, p. 137; Physicsis.com

Index